# The People of Dundee

### Part One
### 1600-1699

### Part Two
### 1700-1799

## *By David Dobson*

**CLEARFIELD**

Copyright © 2009
David Dobson
All Rights Reserved

Part One 1600-1699 originally published
St. Andrews, Fife, Scotland, 2007

Part Two 1700-1799 originally published
St. Andrews, Fife, Scotland, 2008

Reprinted, two parts in one, for
Clearfield Company by
Genealogical Publishing Company
Baltimore, Maryland
2009

ISBN: 978-0-8063-5412-5

*Made in the United States of America*

# INTRODUCTION

Dundee in the seventeenth century was a major port and market town. As a Royal Burgh it was authorised to conduct overseas trade and had developed important economic links with Scandinavia and the Baltic lands, as well as with the Netherlands, France, and Iberia. Dundee has the distinction of being the earliest Scottish ports to have traded with North America, specifically with Newfoundland in 1600 and Virginia in 1627. However emigration to America was minimal as the majority of emigrants headed for continental destinations such as Scandinavia, Poland and the Netherlands.

Since the medieval period Dundee had been semi-autonomous under the control of an elected council. Only the burgesses had the right to elect the burgh council, run businesses, trade, etc, within the burgh. The burgesses, probably less than ten per cent of the male inhabitants, were a self perpetuating minority of the population and comprised of the merchants and the craftsmen of the burgh. Many of them have included in this volume. This publication is designed as an aid to local historians and genealogists wishing to find information on residents of Dundee during the seventeenth century. The references are all based on primary sources mostly located in the National Archives of Scotland in Edinburgh. This book does not claim to be a comprehensive list of Dundee's inhabitants as there are significant sources in the Dundee Archives and Record Centre not used in this compilation.

David Dobson, St Andrews, 2007

**REFERENCES**

DA    =  Dundee Archives
GAR   =  Rotterdam Archives
MSA   =  Maryland State Archives
NAS   =  National Archives of Scotland
RGS   =  Register of the Great Seal of Scotland
RPCS  =  Register of the Privy Council of Scotland
SAB   =  Bergen Archives
DSL   =  Dundee Shipping Lists
LC    =  Laing Charters
WCB   =  Wedderburn's Compt Buik, 1587-1630

## PEOPLE OF DUNDEE

### 1600-1699

**ABBOT, WILLIAM,** a maltman in Dundee, and his spouse Agnes Mullo, testament, 3 May 1686, Comm. Brechin. [NAS]

**ABERCROMBIE, ALEXANDER,** son of Thomas Abercrombie of Gourdie and his wife Grissel Sibbet, settled in Falkenburg in the Duchy of Brandenburg, by 1606. [DA, birthbrief 16.6.1606]

**ABERCROMBIE, Captain ANDREW,** master of the Fox of Dundee, 1612, 1614, 1615; a burgess of Dundee, and his spouse Marion Mudie, died 1629, testament, 14 November 1632, Comm. Brechin. [NAS][DSL][Howff]

**ABERCROMBIE, ANDREW,** a merchant burgess of Dundee, heir to his father Captain Andrew Abercrombie a burgess of Dundee, 1637; husband of Helen Dunmuir, 1637. [NAS.S/H; RS35.S2.I.27]

**ABERCROMBIE, CHRISTINA,** daughter of James Abercrombie a sailor in Dundee, and spouse of James Mudie a sailor there, 1631. [NAS.RS35.S2.VIII.66]

**ABERCROMBIE, HELEN,** daughter of James Abercrombie a sailor in Dundee, 1631. [NAS.RS35.S2.VIII.68]

**ABERCROMBIE, JAMES,** a mariner burgess of Dundee, and his wife Elizabeth Fyffe, 1603; testament, 27 July 1631, Comm. Brechin. [NAS][RGS.VI.1482]

**ABERCROMBIE, JAMES,** a sailor in Dundee, 1631. [NAS.RS35.S1.VIII.66]

**ABERCROMBIE, JOSEPH,** a skipper in Dundee, 1678. [NAS.AC7.4]

**ABERCROMBIE, THOMAS,** a merchant burgess of Dundee, and his spouse Margaret Wemyss, testaments 1 September 1658 and 11 August 1682, Comm. Brechin. [NAS]

**ABERCROMBIE, THOMAS,** a skipper in Dundee, 1699. [NAS.RD4.85.514]

**ABERDEEN, DAVID,** a flesher burgess of Dundee, testament, 21 April 1621, Comm. Brechin. [NAS]

**ABERDEEN, ISOBEL,** spouse to Andrew Hill a baxter burgess of Dundee, testament, 21 April 1621, Comm. Brechin. [NAS]

**ADAMSON, GEORGE,** born 1621, master of the Patience of Dundee, 1679; burgess of Dundee, and his spouse Elspet Brugh, testament, 14 May 1684, Comm. Brechin. [NAS.AC7/5][NAS][Howff]

**ADAMSON, JOHN,** in Dundee, 1612. [DSL]

**AIKMAN, JAMES,** late bailie of Dundee, and his spouse Isobel Bouack, testament, 9 November 1688, Comm. Brechin. [NAS]

**AIR, PATRICK,** sometime of Nether Liff, burgess of Dundee, and his spouse Grizel Strachan, testament, 16 January 1626, Comm. Brechin. [NAS][NAS.RS35.S1.I.127]

**AIRD, JOHN,** a maltman in Dundee, died 1703, husband of Elizabeth Bowman, died 1696. [Howff]

**ALEXANDER, CHRISTIAN,** spouse to Alexander Jack a merchant burgess of Dundee, testament, 26 July 1624, Comm. Brechin. [NAS]

**ALEXANDER, DAVID,** a litster burgess of Dundee, testament, 11 February 1625, Comm. Brechin. [NAS]

**ALEXANDER, THOMAS,** a mariner burgess of Dundee, testament, 22 November 1628, Comm. Brechin. [NAS]

**ALISON, ALEXANDER,** son of the late John Alison, burgess of Dundee, testament, 23 December 1651, Comm. Brechin. [NAS]

**ALISON, ANNA,** spouse to James Boytar, the elder, merchant burgess of Dundee, testament, 28 September 1625, Comm. Brechin. [NAS]

**ALISON, DAVID,** a hammerman burgess of Dundee, and his spouse Janet Hay, testament, 25 April 1611, Comm. Brechin. [NAS]

**ALISON, EUPHEMIA,** 1614; relict of Thomas Auchenleck a former provost of Dundee, 31 March 1635, Comm. Brechin. [NAS][DSL]

**ALISON, ISOBEL,** daughter of the late James Alison former bailie of Dundee, testament, 19 June 1691, Comm. Brechin. [NAS]

**ALISON, JAMES,** son of John Alison, 1612. [WCB#190]

**ALISON, JAMES,** a baxter burgess of Dundee, and his spouse Janet Kyd, testament, 22 March 1634, Comm. Brechin. [NAS]

**ALISON, JAMES,** hospital master of Dundee, 1685; late bailie of Dundee, testament, 9 April 1689, Comm. Brechin. [NAS] [RPCS.XI.62][NAS.RS35.S3.VII.57]

**ALISON, JAMES,** a bailie of Dundee, father of William, Anna, and Margaret, 1688; 1692. [NAS.RD2.69.1034;AC7/9]

**ALISON, JANET,** daughter of the late John Alison, baxter burgess of Dundee, testament, 18 December 1637, Comm. Brechin. [NAS]

**ALLAN, ANDREW,** town councillor of Dundee, 1685; a merchant in Dundee, 1687, 1688. [NAS.AC7/8; RD3.69.29][RPCS.XI.62]

**ALLAN, JAMES,** a weaver on the Hill of Dundee, 1698. [NAS.RS35.S3.X.70]

**ALLAN, WILLIAM,** a mealdealer in Dundee, and his son William, 1650. [NAS.RS35.S2.III.228]

**ANDERSON, ALEXANDER,** in Dundee, 1614. [DSL]

**ANDERSON, ALEXANDER,** a glazier in Dundee, husband of Marie Robertson, born 1660, died 20 December 1696. [Howff]

**ANDERSON, ANDREW,** a weaver on the Hill of Dundee, husband of Margaret Ramsay, 1681. [NAS.RS35.S3.VII.316]

**ANDERSON, ELIZABETH,** daughter of James Anderson a maltman on the Hill of Dundee, 1681. [NAS.RS35.S3.III.376]

**ANDERSON, EUPHAM,** daughter of David Anderson, relict of James Philp a hammerman in Dundee, and spouse of Thomas Millar, 1680. [NAS.RS35.S3.VII.279]

**ANDERSON, GEORGE,** minister of the Second Charge, 1690. [F.5.320]

**ANDERSON, JAMES,** a maltman on the Hill of Dundee, father of James the husband of Marion Mudie, 1692. [NAS.RS35.S3.IX.221]

**ANDERSON, JOHN,** a merchant in Dundee, 1678. [NAS.AC7.4]

**ANDERSON, ROBERT,** in Dundee, 1612. [DSL]

**ANDERSON, WALTER,** burgh officer of Dundee, 1644. [LC#2353]

**ANDREW, ROBERT,** son of Robert Andrew and his wife Eupham Makie in Myreton of Brichty, a weaver in Copenhagen, Denmark, by 1608. [DA, birthbrief, 2.4.1608]

**ANNAN, ALEXANDER,** a merchant in Dundee, husband of Jean daughter of John Smith a tailor there, 1667. [NAS.RS35.S3.III.300, etc]

**ANNAND, ALEXANDER,** a skinner in Dundee, 1611. [RPCS.IX.197]

**ANNAND, JAMES,** son of Alexander Annand a burgess of Dundee, was apprenticed to George Heriot the elder, a goldsmith in Edinburgh, on 22 February 1592. [Edinburgh Register of Apprentices]

7

**ANNAND, JAMES,** in Abbot's Wynd, Dundee, 1600. [RGS.VI.1032]
**ANNAND, THOMAS,** 1613, husband of Elspeth Pearson, 1638. [WCB#186][NAS.RS35.S2.I.290]
**ARBUTHNOT, ALEXANDER,** a bailie of Dundee, 1685, 1688, 1692, 1699. [RPCS.XI.62][NAS.RD2.69.250; AC7/9; RD4.85.287]
**ARBUTHNOT, JOHN,** a merchant burgess of Dundee, testaments 7 February 1666 and 30 January 1683, Comm. Brechin. [NAS]
**ARCHIBALD, ANDREW,** born 1595, surgeon and lithotomist, died 12 September 1662, husband of Catherine Powrie, testament, 1663, Comm. Brechin. [NAS][Howff]
**AUCHENLECK, ANDREW,** born circa 1595, son of John Auchenleck minister of Largo, minister of St Mary's 1642 to 1663, died in April 1663, husband of (1) Janet Lindsay, (2) Margaret Wemyss, (3) Martha Monypenny, (4) Margarte Bower, father of John, Alexander, Andrew, William, David, Katherine, Agnes, Thomas, Charles, Margaret, Euphan, and Lilias. [F.5.316]
**AUCHENLECK, ARCHIBALD,** born 1600, died 27 November 1647, husband of Janet Auchenleck. [Howff]
**AUCHENLECK, ELIZABETH,** heir portioner to her father Alexander Auchinleck a burgess of Dundee, 1627. [NAS.S/H]
**AUCHENLECK, GILBERT,** born 1607, deacon of the bakers, died 25 November 1641. [Howff]
**AUCHENLECK, GILBERT,** deacon of the waulkers of Dundee, 1699. [NAS.RD4.85.435]
**AUCHENLECK, HENRY,** a merchant in Dundee, 1699. [NAS.RD2.82.451; RD4.85.1065]
**AUCHENLECK, HEW,** a merchant burgess of Dundee, 1613. [DSL]
**AUCHENLECK, JOHN,** a merchant burgess of Dundee, 1613, husband of Barbara Traill pre 1620. [DSL][NAS.RS35.S1.I.167]
**AUCHENLECK, MATILDA,** heir portioner to her father Alexander Auchinleck a burgess of Dundee, 1627. [NAS.S/H]
**AUCHENLECK, THOMAS,** a merchant burgess of Dundee, 1612. [DSL]
**AUCHENLECK, THOMAS,** master of the Golden Lion of Dundee, from London to Virginia in 1627. [NA.E190.31.1]
**AUCHENLECK, WILLIAM,** a bailie of Dundee, 1610, Provost in 1614. [RPCS.IX.50][DSL]

**AUCHTERLONY, ANDREW,** born 1627, a lister in Dundee, died 1689, husband of Christian Lyn. [Howff][NAS.RS35.RS35.S2.III.381]
**AUCHTERLONY, JAMES,** 1612. [WCB#187]
**AUCHTERLONY, JOHN,** a merchant in Dundee, 1687. [NAS.AC7/8]
**AUSTIN, PATRICK,** servant of Mr James Dunmuir a notary in Dundee, 1644. [LC#2353]
**BAILLIE, WILLIAM,** a merchant in Dundee, husband of Isobel Thomson, 1694. [NAS.RS35.S3.IV.371]
**BAISLER, ANDREW,** a goldsmith in Dundee, 8 June 1691. [The Nine Trades of Dundee, #151]
**BALBIRNIE, JOHN,** 1612. [WCB#190]
**BALFOUR, ALEXANDER,** a merchant in Dundee, 1699. [NAS.RD4.84.578]
**BALFOUR, DAVID,** in Argyll Street, Dundee, 1621, son and heir of the late John Balfour, son of the late David Balfour of Balledmonth. [LC#1891]
**BALLINGALL, JOHN,** a merchant in Dundee, 1699. [NAS.RD4.84.640]
**BALMANNO, PETER,** a merchant burgess of Dundee, 1613. [DSL]
**BALNEAVES, PATRICK,** a bailie of Dundee, 1685; a merchant in Dundee, 1688.[RPCS.XI.62][NAS.RD3.68.527]
**BALVAIRD, ROBERT,** a merchant in Dundee, 1699. [NAS.RD2.82.136; RD3.92.355]
**BARCLAY, OLIVER,** a merchant in Dundee, 1699. [NAS.RD4.84.640]
**BARCLAY, PATRICK,** a maltman in Dundee, husband of Isabel Lindsay, 1649. [NAS.RS35.S2.III.152]
**BARKER, ANNA,** relict of Francis Steuart in Dundee, 1699. [NAS.RD4.84.814]
**BARNET, JOHN,** a saddler in Dundee, husband of Margaret Mudie, 1673. [NAS.RS35.S3.V.194]
**BARNS, EUPHAN,** in Dundee, 1612. [RPCS.IX.385]
**BARRY, JAMES,** in Dundee, 1597. [WCB#186]
**BARRIE, JAMES,** a bonnetmaker on the Hill of Dundee, 1642 [NAS.RS35.S2.II.57]
**BARRY, JOHN,** heir to his father William Barry a merchant burgess of Dundee, 1617. [NAS.S/H]

**BARRY, JAMES,** born 1580, a bonnetmaker burgess in Dundee, 1597, died 20 November 1645, father of James. [WCB#186][Howff]

**BARRIE, RICHARD,** a burgess of Dundee, 1637. [NAS.RS35.S2.I.7]

**BATHGATE, ANDREW,** a maltman and merchant in Dundee, husband of Elizabeth Reid, 1676. [NAS.AC7.4; RS35.S3.VI.434]

**BAXTER, JOHN,** a Baxter burgess, died 20 October 1609, husband of Helena Seyton. [Howff]

**BAXTER, JOHN,** a tailor in Dundee, 1612. [RPCS.IX.385]

**BATHGATE, JOHN,** a notary public in Dundee, husband of Janet Jack, father of Andrew a merchant there, 1631. [NAS.RS35.S1.VIII.260]

**BAXTER, ALEXANDER,** a shipmaster in Dundee, 1637. [NAS.RS35.S2.I.46]

**BAXTER, PATRICK,** a merchant in Dundee, 1629. [NAS.AC7.2.132]

**BEATON, JAMES,** doctor of medicine, and Janet Goldman his spouse, in Flukergate, Dundee, 1644. [LC#2352]

**BEATON, JOHN,** Collector of Customs at Dundee, 1699. [NAS.RD2.82.620]

**BEATON, THOMAS,** a skipper in Broughty Ferry, husband of Margaret Knight, parents of David a sailor there, 1668. [NAS.RS35.S3.IV.378]

**BELL, ALEXANDER,** a merchant in Dundee, husband of Margaret Lennox, 1688. [NAS.RD4.63.474; RS35.S3.VIII.314]]

**BELL, AGNES,** heir to David Hoppringill a burgess of Dundee, 1628. [NAS.S/H]

**BEVOC, THOMAS,** born 1587, a merchant burgess, died 17 November 1642. [Howff]

**BLACK, ANDREW,** 1611. [WCB#189]

**BLACK, BESSIE,** in Dundee, 1612. [RPCS.IX.385]

**BLACK, JOHN,** a merchant burgess, died 5 May 1633, husband of Elspet Pirie, testament, 1634, Comm. Brechin. [NAS][Howff][NAS.RS35.S2.I.7]

**BLACK, WALTER,** in Dundee, 1611. [RGS.VI.464]

**BLAIR, ALEXANDER,** master of the Grace of Dundee, 1614. [DSL]

**BLAIR, ALEXANDER,** Dean of Guild of Dundee, and co-owner of the James of Dundee, 1692, 1699. [NAS.AC7/9; RD2.82.321] [RPCS.XI.62]

**BLAIR, WILLIAM,** born 1629, a merchant burgess of Dundee, died 14 March 1693. [Howff]
**BLAKE, JAMES,** born 1553, a merchant burgess, died 13 January 1609, husband of Catherine Davidson. [Howff]
**BLAKIE, ANDREW,** a bonnet-maker in Dundee, 1612. [RPCS.IX.385]
**BLYTH, ALEXANDER,** born 1580, a skipper burgess of Dundee, died 4 February 1644, husband of Euphemia Wedderburn, born 1565, died 24 October 1643, testament, 1625, Comm. Brechin. [NAS][Howff]
**BLYTH, WILLIAM,** a skipper, husband of Eufame Ramsay, born 1584, died 27 August 1613. [Howff]
**BOWEN, JAMES,** a merchant in Dundee, husband of Elizabeth Blair, steward on the Hope, to Darien 1699. [NAS.GD406,162, C39/21; CC8.8.84]
**BOWER, ALEXANDER,** a merchant burgess of Dundee, 1614, 1621. [RGS.VIII.1648][DSL]
**BOWER, JAMES,** merchant burgess of Dundee, husband of Bessie Bruce (born 1574, died 15 May 1640), father of Barbara Bower, testament, 1628, Comm. Brechin. [NAS][Howff]
**BOWER, JAMES,** town councillor of Dundee, 1685. [RPCS.XI.62]
**BOWER, JOHN,** a weaver on the Hill of Dundee, husband of Margaret, daughter of John Shanks a weaver, 1692. [NAS.RS35.S3.IX.46, etc]
**BOWER, THOMAS,** born 1553, a skinner burgess of Dundee, died in October 1603, husband of Janet Couttie. [Howff]
**BOWER, THOMAS,** a merchant in Dundee, 1679, 1699. [NAS.AC7/5; RD2.82.620]
**BOWER, RODGER,** a skinner burgess in Dundee, 1611, 1613, died 2 March 1628. [RPCS.IX.197][DSL][Howff]
**BOYACK, JOHN,** a maltman burgess of Dundee, husband of Isobel Gourlay born 1663, died 1 June 1669, testament, 1670, Comm. Brechin. [NAS][Howff]
**BOYACK, JOHN,** a maltman burgess of Dundee, husband of Elizabeth Kirkland, born 1668, died 22 December 1694. [Howff]
**BOYACK, JOHN,** the younger, a merchant in Dundee, 1699. [NAS.RD4.84.691; RD4.85.541]
**BOYACK, THOMAS,** a skinner in Dundee, 1611. [RPCS.IX.197]
**BOYD, ANDREW,** in 1621. [WCB#185]
**BOYTAR, ALEXANDER,** a skinner in Dundee, 1611. [RPCS.IX.197]

**BOYTAR, ANDREW,** a merchant burgess of Dundee, 1621. [RGS.VIII.1648]

**BOYTAR, JAMES,** a merchant burgess of Dundee, 1612, auditor, 1614, [DSL]; of Nether Liff, senior, a burgess of Dundee, granted his lands to his son James and his future bride Margaret, daughter of Robert Clayhills a bailie burgess of Dundee in 1621. [RGS.VIII.1648]

**BOYTAR, JAMES,** of Netherliff, heir to James Boytar the elder, bailie of Dundee, 1647. [NAS.S/H]

**BOYTAR, THOMAS,** bailie of Dundee, 1620. [RGS.VIII.1989]

**BRISBANE, JAMES,** heir to his father James Brisbane, Mains of Dudhope, parish of Dundee, 16 June 1655. [NAS.S/H]

**BROWN, ALEXANDER,** a baxter burgess of Dundee, husband of Margaret Drummond, parents of William born 1603, died in August 1619, testament 1625, Comm. Brechin. [NAS][Howff]

**BROWN, ALEXANDER,** born 1592, a maltman burgess, died 22 June 1646. [Howff]

**BROWN, DAVID,** a tailor in Dundee, husband of Elizabeth, daughter of David Williamson a tailor on the Hill of Dundee, 1655. [NAS.RS35.S2.V.1]

**BROWN, DAVID,** a merchant in Dundee, 1699. [NAS.RD2.82.1]

**BROWN, GEORGE,** born 1591, bailie of Dundee, died 6 October 1651. [Howff]

**BROWN, GEORGE,** a merchant burgess and provost of Dundee, husband of Grissill Scott, born 1630, died 1667, heir to her father Thomas Scott bailie of Dundee, 1 May 1662; a bailie of Dundee, 1661, testament, 1667, Comm. Brechin. [NAS.S/H; RD3.2.449; RS35.S3.III.245] [Howff]

**BROWN, GEORGE,** a merchant in Dundee, 1699. [NAS.RD4.85.1121]

**BROWN, JAMES,** a wright burgess of Dundee, died 1622. [Howff]

**BROWN, JOHN,** a merchant in Dundee, 1678. [NAS.AC7.4]

**BROWN, JOHN,** born 1645, a shoemaker burgess of Dundee, died 7 April 1691. [Howff]

**BROWN, THOMAS,** a wheelwright in Dundee, husband of Barbara Lowson, testament, 1632, Comm. Brechin. [NAS][Howff]

**BRUCE, JOHN,** a merchant in Dundee, 1676. [NAS.AC7.4]

**BRUCE, HELENA,** heir portioner to her father Robert Bruce the younger of Pitlethie, in the lands of Wallace-Craigie, Dundee, 1623. [NAS.S/H]

**BRUCE, MARGARET,** heir portioner to her father Robert Bruce the younger of Pitlethie, in the lands of Wallace-Craigie, Dundee, 1623. [NAS.S/H]

**BRUGH, JAMES,** a skipper in Dundee, 1691. [NAS.AC7/9]

**BUICK, JAMES,** a burgess of Dundee, 1612. [RPCS.IX.50]

**BULTIE, ROBERT,** born 1553, a merchant burgess, died 1611. [Howff]

**BULTIE, ROBERT,** a merchant bailie of Dundee, husband of Elizabeth Rollo, 1656. [NAS.RS35.S3.V.130]

**BURGH, PATRICK,** a skinner in Dundee, 1611. [RPCS.IX.197]

**BURGH, WILLIAM,** son of William Burgh of Craigie and his wife Janet Gellatly, settled in Konigsberg by 1612. [DA.birthbrief, 17.8.1612]

**BURNS, JAMES,** born 1615, a maltman burgess of Dundee, died 26 December 1664, husband of Elisabeth Bowman, testament, 1665, Comm. Brechin. [NAS][Howff]

**BURSIE, ROBERT,** in 1613. [WCB#185]

**CAMPBELL, GEORGE,** servant to Thomas Wichtan a notary in Dundee, 1621. [RGS.VIII.1648]

**CANDOW, ROBERT,** born 1559, a merchant burgess of Dundee, died 26 August 1620, husband of Marion Bower born 1574, died 28 August 1606, testament, 1621/1622, Comm. Brechin. [NAS][Howff]

**CARGILL, MARGARET,** relict of John Meall a master of the English School of Dundee, testament, 20 July 1698, Comm. Brechin. [NAS]

**CARMICHAEL, DAVID,** son of the late Patrick Carmichael a burgess of Dundee heir to James Carmichael his grandfather, 17 December 1657. [NAS.S/H]

**CARMICHAEL, JOHN,** a soldier from Dundee, married Anneken Jans in Heusden, the Netherlands, on 18 May 1636. [Heusden Marriage Register]

**CARMICHAEL, ROBERT,** master of the Hopewell of Dundee, 1614. [DSL]

**CARMICHAEL, WILLIAM,** a skinner in Dundee, 1611. [RPCS.IX.197]

**CARMICHAEL, WILLIAM,** a merchant burgess of Dundee, 1613. [DSL]

**CASKE, JAMES,** born 1594, a maltman burgess of Dundee, died 1630, husband of Agnes Whittet. [Howff]

**CHALMERS, EDWARD,** dead by 1612. [WCB#186]
**CHALMERS, PATRICK,** master of the Fortune of Dundee, 1614. [DSL]
**CHAPLIN, GEORGE,** a maltman burgess in Friar's Wynd, Dundee, husband of (1) Agnes Dorward born 1557, died 24 October 1603, (2) Margaret Lochmalownie, testament, 1605, 1609, Comm. Brechin. [NAS][Howff]
**CHAPLIN, GEORGE,** burgh officer of Dundee, 1621. [LC#1891]
**CHAPLIN, WILLIAM,** a skinner in Dundee, 1611. [RPCS.IX.197]
**CHRISTIE, ROBERT,** a cordiner in Dundee, husband of Helen Stratton, 1693. [NAS.RS35.S3.IX.259]
**CLAYHILLS, PETER,** husband of Margaret Wedderburn, born 1552, died 20 September 1617. [Howff]
**CLAYHILLS, ROBERT,** bailie of Dundee, 1609, burgess 1612, kirkmaster, 1614. [WCB#187][DSL]
**CLERK, ANDREW,** born 1632, glazier, died 1694, husband of Catherine Stevinson who died 1694. [Howff]
**CLERK, JAMES,** in Dundee, 1614. [DSL]
**CLERK, JOHN,** a merchant in Dundee, 1661. [NAS.RD3.2.360]
**COCHRANE, JAMES,** a merchant burgess of Dundee, husband of Margaret Paterson born 1594, died 30 March 1628. [Howff]
**COCKBURN, ALEXANDER,** a merchant burgess of Dundee, 1612, 1613, piermaster of Dundee, 1614. [RPCS.IX.50][DSL]
**COCKBURN, DAVID,** Flukergait, Dundee, 1601. [RGS.VI.1187]
**COLENE, ALEXANDER,** in Cowgait, Dundee, 1600. [RGS.VI.1060]
**COLEN, DAVID,** born 1587, a merchant burgess of Dundee, died in April 1635, husband of Elspet Lovell, testament, 1635, Comm. Brechin. [NAS][Howff]
**COLLACE, ANDREW,** minister of St Mary's, 1635 to 1639. [F.5.315]
**COLVILL, JOHN,** a merchant in Dundee, husband of Euphan Man, 1676. [NAS.RS35.S3.VI.96]
**CONSTABLE, THOMAS,** a maltman in Dundee, husband of Catharine Shear, 1666. [NAS.RS35.S3.III.64]
**COOK, JOHN,** born 1631, a merchant burgess, died 1 January 1681, husband of Elizabeth Grym, testament, 1683, Comm. Brechin. [NAS][Howff]
**COOK, WILLIAM,** in Dundee, 1614. [DSL]

**COPPINE, NINIAN,** a mariner burgesss of Dundee, 1612, testament, 1623, Comm. Brechin, husband of Christian Kynneris, born 1551, died 25 December 1615. [DSL][NAS][Howff]

**COPPING, ALEXANDER,** a merchant sailor of Dundee, husband of Isobel Pearson, 1638. [NAS.RS35.S2.I.175]

**CORSAR, PATRICK,** master of the Providence of Dundee, 1680. [NAS.AC7/5]

**COULL, THOMAS,** a barber in Dundee, 1679. [NAS.AC7/5]

**COUPER, WALTER,** born 1576, a tailor, died 25 December 1628, husband of Janet Mortimer. [Howff]

**COUTIE, ALEXANDER,** born 1557, a merchant burgess of Dundee, died April 1625, husband of Agnes Murrison, testament, 1636, Comm. Brechin. [NAS][Howff]

**COUTIE, JAMES,** born 1532, a merchant burgess of Dundee, died 22 February 1604. [Howff]

**COWIE, ANDREW,** born 1554, a merchant burgess of Dundee, died 12 November 1608, testament, 1609, Comm. Edinburgh. [NAS][Howff]

**CRAIG, JOHN,** a bonnetmaker on the Hill of Dundee, son of Elspeth Low, 1639. [NAS.RS35.S2.I.488]

**CRAWFORD, HENRY,** of Seaton, born 1628, a merchant and bailie of Dundee, died 19 July 1684, husband of Margaret Dunmuir. [Howff]

**CROB, JAMES,** in Argyll's Gait, Dundee, 1611. [RGS.VI.464]

**CROCKAT, COLIN,** master of the Swan of Dundee, 1614. [DSL]

**CROCKAT, GEORGE,** a merchant in Dundee, 1688. [NAS.RD4.63.857]

**CROMBIE, THOMAS,** a merchant burgess of Dundee, 1612. [DSL]

**CROY, JOHN,** a merchant in Dundee, husband of Margaret, sister of William Shearer a merchant there, 1693. [NAS.RS35.S3.IX.274]

**DAVIDSON, GEORGE,** a merchant in Dundee, 1679. [NAS.AC7/5]

**DAVIDSON, RICHARD,** in Argyll Street, Dundee, 1621, son and heir of James Davidson a merchant burgess of Dundee

**DAVIDSON, RICHARD,** a merchant burgess, dead by 1674, husband of Catherine Man died 17 September 1677, testament, 1674, Comm. Brechin. [NAS][Howff]

**DAVIDSON, ROBERT,** a merchant burgess of Dundee, 1613, 1621, husband of Margaret Watson born 1564, died 16 April 1640. [DSL][RGS.VIII.1648][Howff]

**DAVIDSON, ROBERT,** of Balgay, born 1600, a merchant, died 24 July 1665, relict Grissel Bowman died 1681. [Howff]

**DAVIDSON, THOMAS,** master of the <u>Allan of Dundee</u>, 1614. [DSL]

**DAVIDSON, WILLIAM,** the elder, merchant burgess of Dundee, born 1569, died 18 January 1617. [Howff]

**DAVIDSON, WILLIAM,** burgess of Dundee, spouse of Elizabeth Goldman, 1644. [LC#2352]

**DAVIDSON, WILLIAM,** a maltman burgess of Dundee, husband of Janet Smyth, born 1613, died 15 August 1649. [Howff]

**DAVIDSON, WILLIAM,** a baxter in Dundee, 1688. [NAS.RD2.59.500]

**DEWAR, JOHN,** a weaver on the Hill of Dundee, husband of Anna Smith relict of Alexander Jack, 1698. [NAS.RS35.S3.X.72]

**DICK, JAMES,** a writer in Dundee, died 1699, husband of Christian Chalmers, died 1737, testament, 1699, Comm. Brechin. [NAS][Howff]

**DICK, WILLIAM,** in Dundee, 1614. [DSL]

**DISHINGTON, JOHN,** a skipper in Dundee, husband of Agnes Nicol, 1639. [NAS.RS35.S2.I.512]

**DOIG, JANET,** daughter of Thomas Doig a merchant burgess of Dundee, wife of William Fendat burgess of Dundee, heir to Catherine Doig, daughter of John Doig, mariner burgess of Dundee,1629. [NAS.S/H]

**DOIG, THOMAS,** a maltman in Dundee, 1688. [NAS.RD2.69.500]

**DONALDSON, ANDREW,** a merchant in Dundee, 1613. [DSL]

**DONALDSON, JOHN,** son of Archibald Donaldson and his wife Christian Ferrier, settled in Prussia by 1610. [DA, birthbrief, 26.6.1606]

**DONALDSON, JOHN,** in Balgray, heir to Matthew Donaldson a fuller burgess of Dundee, 1622. [NAS.S/H]

**DONALDSON, WILLIAM,** skipper in Dundee, husband of Elizabeth Gray, 1697. [NAS.RD3.87.364]

**DORWARD, GEORGE,** 1613, first husband of Bessie Bruce born 1574, died 15 May 1640, testament, 1627, Comm. Brechin. [WCB#186][NAS][Howff]

**DOUGLAS, GEORGE,** a litster in Dundee, husband of Elizabeth Shear, 1666. [NAS.RS35.S3.III.64]

**DOUGLAS, JAMES,** chamberlain to Viscount Dudhope, 1656. [LC#2496]

**DOWIE, JOHN,** born 1646, a shipmaster in Dundee, died in January 1721, husband of Christian Urquhart, born 1659, died in December 1717. [Howff]

**DRUMMOND, DAVID,** town councillor of Dundee, 1685; a merchant in Dundee and co-owner of the James of Dundee, 1692. [NAS.AC7/9] [RPCS.XI.62]

**DRUMMOND, ISOBEL,** on the Hill of Dundee, 1699. [NAS.RD4/85/754]

**DRUMMOND, THOMAS,** born 1615, a skipper in Dundee, died 18 October 1671, husband of Helen Luke, born 1614, died 1669. [Howff]

**DRUMMOND, WILLIAM,** a soldier from Dundee, married Adriaenke Adriaens in Dordrecht, the Netherlands, on 22 March 1587. [Dordrecht Marriage Register]

**DRUMMOND, WILLIAM,** born 1643, died 1 August 1700, husband of Sarah Bell, born 1663, died 11 December 1714. [Howff]

**DRYMIE, JOHN,** a tailor in Dundee, 1612. [RPCS.IX.385]

**DUFF, WILLIAM,** born pre 1570, a maltman burgess of Dundee, died 1620, husband of Magdalene Edeson. [Howff]

**DUKE, ROBERT,** a tailor in Dundee, 1612. [RPCS.IX.385]

**DUNBAR, DAVID,** a merchant in Dundee, died 2 May 1723.[Howff]

**DUNBAR, WILLIAM,** a merchant in Dundee, husband of Janet Liddell, born 1605, died 29 September 1649. [Howff]

**DUNCAN, ALEXANDER,** a goldsmith, son of Finlay Duncan a surgeon, was admitted as a burgess of Dundee on 19 March 1611. [DBR]

**DUNCAN, ALEXANDER,** from Dundee, a seaman in Dutch service 1641, a skipper in 1647. [GAR.ONA.202.64.87/ONA.335.218.535]

**DUNCAN, ALEXANDER,** of Lundie, born 1652, died April 1696, wife Ann Drummond, born 1653, died April 1695.[AHowff]

**DUNCAN, JANET,** mother of Thomas Bower a merchant in Dundee, 1688. [NAS.RD4.62.419]

**DUNCAN, JOHN,** son of John Duncan, a mariner, and his wife Bessie Vauss, a traveller in Prussia by 1607. [DA, birthbrief, 13.7.1607]

**DUNCAN, JOHN,** a mariner burgess of Dundee, husband of Marion Kinneris, born 1570, died 2 April 1637, testament, 1637, Comm. Brechin. [NAS][Howff]

**DUNCAN, JOHN,** in Dundee, 1612, 1613. [DSL]

**DUNCAN, JOHN,** born 159-, a merchant burgess of Dundee, died 16 October 1637, husband of Isobel Cockburn, testament, 1637, Comm. Brechin. [NAS][Howff]

**DUNCAN, JOHN,** born 1676, son of Alexander Duncan of Lundie, died in July 1696. [Howff]

**DUNCAN, JOHN,** a merchant in Dundee, 1688. [NAS.RD3.68.180]

**DUNCAN, JOHN,** formerly a bailie of Dundee in 1685, co-owner of the James of Dundee, 1692. [RPCS.XI.62][NAS.AC7/9]

**DUNCAN, THOMAS,** a merchant in Dundee, 1686. [NAS.AC7/7]

**DUNCAN, WALTER,** in Dundee, 1613. [DSL]

**DUNCAN, WILLIAM,** born 1556, a physician burgess of Dundee, died May 1608, husband of Katherine Wedderburn who died 160-. [Howff]

**DUNCANSON, JOHN,** minister of South Kirk from 1624 to 1652(?). [F.5.319]

**DUNMUIR, JAMES,** writer in Dundee, 1644. [LC#2352]

**DURWARD, GEORGE,** 1613. [WCB#186]

**DYNNIS, JOHN,** a hammerman and swordslipper burgess of Dundee, died in October 1603, relict Elspet Wilkieson, testament, 16 January 1626, Comm. Brechin. [NAS]

**EDWARD, ALEXANDER,** a merchant burgess of Dundee, 1612, 1613, 1615. [DSL]

**EDWARD, ALEXANDER,** junior, a merchant burgess of Dundee, husband of Elizabeth Lochmalony, testament, 1632, Comm. Brechin. [NAS][Howff]

**FAIRN, JOHN,** a baker in Dundee, 1612. [RPCS.IX.385]

**FAIRNEY, GEORGE,** a merchant in Dundee, husband of Martha Scott, 1667. [NAS.RS35.S3.III.245]

**FAIRWEATHER, GEORGE,** born 1651, son of William Fairweather, master of the Good Intention of Dundee, 1678; master of the Unity of Dundee sailing to Sweden an the Netherlands in the 1680s, died 25 May 1683, testament, 1684, Comm. Brechin. [NAS.AC7.4; E727.6/8/9][Howff gravestone]

**FAIRWEATHER, THOMAS,** a merchant in Dundee and factor for the Presbytery thereof, 1699. [NAS.RD3/83/220, etc]

**FAIRWEATHER, WILLIAM,** born 1622, skipper in Dundee, master of the Thomas of Dundee voyaging to Scandinavia and the Baltic in 1660s, husband of (1) Christian Gray, (2) Janet Morris, died on 13 May 1683; testament, 8 October 1684. Comm. Brechin. [NAS][Howff gravestone][NAS.E72.7.1]

**FAIRWEATHER, WILLIAM,** skipper in Dundee, 1699; master of the Margaret of Dundee bound for Darien in January 1700. [NAS.RD4/84/505; GD406]

**FEATHIE, HENRY,** a merchant in Dundee, 1680. [NAS.AC7/5]

**FEATHIE, JOHN,** a merchant in Dundee, husband of Margaret Strachan, 1653. [NAS.RS35.S2.IV.254]

**FELL, WILLIAM,** a flesher burgess of Dundee, husband of Matilda Peirson, testament, 1610, Comm. Brechin. [NAS]

**FENTON, JOHN,** a burgess of Dundee, 1612. [RPCS.IX.50]

**FERGUSON, Mr JAMES,** of Dundee Grammar School, 30 July 1605. [RPCS.VI.206]

**FERGUSON, JOHN,** merchant, husband of Catherine Guthrie born 1639, died 20 January 1668. [Howff]

**FERGUSON, WILLIAM,** bailie of Dundee, 1610, Dean of Guild in 1614. [RPCS.IX.50][DSL]

**FERGUSON, WILLIAM,** born 1563, a physician and burgess of Dundee, died 25 March 1627, husband of Euphemia Kinloch, born 1573, died 6 June 1630. [Howff]

**FERNES, JOHN,** a burgess of Dundee, 1612. [RPCS.IX.50]

**FIFE, ROBERT,** from Dundee, a burgess of Bergen, Norway, in 1631, dead by 1642. [SAB]

**FINDLAYSON, JOHN,** a bailie and burgess of Dundee, 1600; burgh auditor, 1614. [SHS.4/2/X.68][DSL]

**FLEMING, ALEXANDER,** born 1662, a maltman burgess, died 24 December 1710, husband of Agnes Mullow. [Howff][NAS.RS35.S3.IX.562]

**FLEMING, DAVID,** a maltman in Dundee, 1639. [NAS.RS35.S2.I.413]

**FLEMING, THOMAS,** a maltman burgess, died 14 February 1614, his wife Elspet Pattullo died 17 July 1617. [Howff]

**FLEMING, THOMAS,** a maltman in Dundee, 1637. [NAS.RS35.S2.I.42]

**FLESHER, DAVID,** merchant burgess of Dundee, 1610. [RPCS.IX.97]

**FLETCHER, ANDREW,** a mariner in Dundee, 1629. [NAS.AC7.2.153]

**FLETCHER, JAMES,** in Dundee, 1614. [DSL]

**FLETCHER, JAMES,** provost of Dundee and co-owner of the James of Dundee, 1685, 1688, 1692, 1697. [NAS.RD3.68.179; AC7/9; RD3.88.89; RD2.81.1.5][RPCS.XI.62]

**FLETCHER, ROBERT,** deacon of the merchants' guild of Dundee, 1601, 1614. [RGS.VI.1190][DSL]

**FLETCHER, ROBERT,** of Easter Innerpeffer, merchant and provost of Dundee, husband of Janet Pearson, 1638. [NAS.RS35.S2.I.290]

**FLETCHER, ROBERT,** provost of Dundee, 1697. [NAS.RD4.81.713]

**FLEMING, THOMAS,** a merchant burgess of Dundee, died 10 September 1707. [Howff]

**FORATH, Captain ALEXANDER,** from Dundee, an officer of the Swedish Navy from 1611 to 1627, in Nygranden, Stockholm, 1618, killed in 1627. [NAS.GD334.114/116]

**FORD, JAMES,** skinner in Dundee, 1611. [RPCS.IX.197]

**FORREST, THOMAS,** a pewterer, husband of Christian Webster, born 1672, died 1710. [Howff]

**FORRESTER, ANDREW,** from Dundee, a Lieutenant on Sir William Alexander's expedition to Nova Scotia, Commander of Port Royal there in 1629, captured by the French and taken to England in 1633; as agent for Sir William Alexander, Earl of Stirling, he claimed Long Island, New York, on his behalf from the Dutch, there in September 1647. [DCB][NYHM.Dutch#IV.442-446]

**FORRESTER, ANDREW,** born 1637, bailie of Dundee, died 13 November 1671, husband of Marjory Watson who died in 1708. [Howff]

**FORRESTER, GEORGE,** born 1635, dean of Guild, died 3 January 1675, husband of Martha, and father of Alexander, testament, 1692, Comm. Brechin, [NAS][Howff]

**FORRESTER, JAMES,** in Dundee, 1601, natural son of Mr Andrew Forrester rector of Kinmoir. [RGS.VI.1187]

**FORRESTER, JOHN,** auditor, 1614. [DSL]

**FORRESTER, ROBERT,** master of the Angel of Dundee, 1614. [DSL]

**FORRESTER, ROBERT,** skipper and timmerman burgess, husband of Agnes Scott born 1616, died 11 November 1669, testament, 1635, Comm. Brechin. [NAS][Howff]

**FORSYTH, JOHN,** a merchant in Dundee, husband of Margaret Rankine, 1661. [NAS.RD2.1.693]

**FOTHERINGHAM, CHARLES,** in Dundee, 1614. [DSL]

**FOTHERINGHAM, JOHN,** son and heir of John Fotheringham, burgess of Dundee, was granted the Cross House and garden, Flukergait, Dundee, 1601. [RGS.VI.1187]

**FRASER, ROBERT,** born 1553, a merchant burgess, died 30 March 1628, husband of Janet Philip, testament, 1628, Comm. Brechin. [NAS][Howff]

**FRASER, THOMAS,** a soldier from Dundee, married Lubberich Reyers in Harderwijk, the Netherlands, on 15 February 1607. [Harderwijk Marriage Register]

**FULLERTON, GEORGE,** of Wester Denoon, barony of Dundee, and his wife Matilda Neva, 1608. [RGS.VI.2083]

**FULLERTON, THOMAS,** an auditor, 1614. [DSL]

**FUTHIE, HENRY,** a litster in Dundee, husband of Isabel McFarlane, 1648. [NAS.RS35.S2.III.151]

**FUTHIE, JAMES,** a skinner in Dundee, husband of Anna Thain, 1638. [NAS.RS35.S2.I.298]

**FYFFE, JOHN,** in Dundee, 1600. [RGS.VI.1032]

**FYFFE, MARGARET,** resident of St Margaret's Close, Dundee, 1612. [WCB#187]

**FYFFE, ROBERT,** from Dundee, a burgess of Bergen, Norway, in 1631, dead by 1642. [SAB]

**FYFFE, THOMAS,** servant to Alexander Wedderburn town clerk of Dundee, 1619. [RGS.VIII.117]

**GARDYNE, GEORGE,** master of the Allan of Dundee, 1614. [DSL]

**GARDYN, JAMES,** deacon of the bonnetmakers of Dundee, 1611. [RPCS.IX.197]

**GARDYN, PATRICK,** deacon of the skinners of Dundee, 1611. [RPCS.IX.197]

**GARDYNE, PATRICK,** a goldsmith in Dundee, 1624. ['The Nine Trades of Dundee, #149]

**GARDYNE, PATRICK,** in Crawford's Lands, Dundee, 1666. [RGS.XI.883]

**GARDYNE, ROBERT,** a goldsmith, son of Robert Gardyne a merchant, was admitted as a burgess of Dundee on 12 October 1624. [DBR]

**GARDYNE, ROBERT,** a merchant in Dundee, husband of Janet, daughter of James Thom a merchant in Dundee, 1681]

**GARDYN, THOMAS,** a burgess of Dundee, 1612. [RPCS.IX.50]

**GAIRIE, or GARVIE, GEORGE,** a merchant burgess of Dundee, husband of Isobel Davidson, born 1607, died 25 February 1641, testament, 1641, Comm. Brechin. [NAS][Howff]

**GARIOCH, GEORGE,** a merchant in Dundee, husband of Agnes Paton, 1642. [NAS.RS35.S2.II.65]

**GARIOCH, MARGARET,** spouse to James Mudie a husbandman in Craigie, Dundee, testament, 20 July 1597, Comm. St Andrews. [NAS]

**GEIKIE, DAVID,** a maltman burgess of Dundee, husband of Isobel Crichton, born 1683, died 31 October 1714. [Howff]

**GELLATLY, JOHN,** son of Walter Gellatly and his wife Janet Smart, a traveller in Mehlsack, Koningsberg, 1608. [DA, birthbrief, 28.4.1608]

**GELLATLY, THOMAS,** son of George Gellatly and his wife Katherine Man, settled in Danzig by 1615. [DA, birthbrief, 28.4.1615]

**GEMMILL, ANDREW,** born 1596, merchant and hospital master, died in August 1638, husband of Helen Gray, testament, 1640, Comm. Brechin. [Howff]

**GEORGESON, GEORGE,** from Dundee, a burgess of Bergen, Norway, 1615. [SAB]

**GEORGESON, JOHN,** from Dundee, a burgess of Bergen, Norway, 1615. [SAB]

**GIBB, JOHN,** a bonnetmaker in Dundee, 1612. [RPCS.IX.385]

**GIBB, WILLIAM,** born 1567, resident of Lochton, died 10 May 1645. [Howff]

**GIBB, WILLIAM,** a bonnetmaker on the Hill of Dundee, husband of Margaret Whitton, 1684. [NAS.RS35.S3.VIII.186]

**GIBSON, JAMES,** born in Dundee around 1618, arrived in Amsterdam in 1647 aboard the Ostrich from the East Indies. [GAR.ONA.209.11.26]

**GIBSON, JAMES,** a baker in Dundee, 1638. [NAS.RS35.S2.I.308]

**GIBSON, JAMES,** a flesher on the Hill of Dundee, husband of Elspeth, daughter of Patrick Simpson there, 1673. [NAS.RS35.S3.V.274]

**GIBSON, JOHN,** a baker in Dundee, husband of Janet Dickison, 1637. [NAS.RS35.S2.I.6]

**GIBSON, ROBERT,** son of Alexander Gibson a baker on the Hill of Dundee, uncle to Thomas Gibson a baker in Dundee, 1637. [NAS.RS35.S2.I.308, etc]

GIBSON, THOMAS, a baxter in Dundee, husband of Margaret Shear, 1638. [NAS.RS35.S2.I.309]
GLEG, JAMES, a merchant in Dundee, spouse of Janet Wichton, 1661. [NAS.RS35.S3.I.70]
GLENNY, RICHARD, a maltman in Dundee, husband of Elizabeth Masterton, 1649. [NAS.RS35.S2.III.262]
GLYGE, Mr JAMES, a schoolmaster in Dundee, 1631. [NAS.GD48, Box 4/199]
GOLDMAN, CHARLES, a merchant in Dundee, 1621. [NAS.RS35.S1.I.181]
GOLDMAN, ELIZABETH, daughter of William Goldman of Flashill, spouse of William Davidson a merchant in Dundee, 1638. [NAS.RS35.S2.I.210, etc]
GOLDMAN, JAMES, born 1590, a merchant burgess of Dundfee, died in September 1632, testament, 1633, Comm. Edinburgh; husband of Margaret Ogilvy. [NAS][Howff]
GOLDMAN, JAMES, a burgess of Dundee, 1648. [NAS.RS35.S2.III.279]
GOLDMAN, JANET, daughter of William Goldman of Flashill, spouse of James Beaton a doctor of medicine in Perth, 1649. [NAS.RS35.S2.III.321, etc]
GOLDMAN, JOHN, born 1531, a merchant burgess of Dundee, died 3 April 1605, testament, 1608, Comm. Edinburgh; husband of Christian Man, born 1567, died 8 September 1603. [Howff][NAS]
GOLDMAN, JOHN, born 1573, a merchant, died in September 1607, husband of Elisabeth Traill, born 1578, died in September 1607, testament, 1608, Comm. Edinburgh. [Howff][NAS]
GOLDMAN, MARGARET, daughter of William Goldman of Flashill, bailie of Dundee, and spouse of James Rollok of Monksholm, a merchant of Dundee, 1649. [NAS.RS35.S2.III.321, etc]
GOLDMAN, MARION, daughter of William Goldman of Flashill, spouse of Captain Patrick Campbell, brother of Colin Campbell of Lundie, 1649. [NAS.RS35.S2.III.321, etc]
GOLDMAN, ROBERT, a skinner in Dundee, 1611. [RPCS.IX.197]; died 1617(?). [Howff]
GOLDMAN, THOMAS, in Dundee, 1612. [RPCS.IX.385]
GOLDMAN, WILLIAM, of Sandford, born 1570, bailie of Dundee, 1608/9, died 4 April 1613. [WCB#187/189][Howff]

**GOLDMAN, WILLIAM,** of Flashill, bailie and burgess of Dundee, in Flukergate, Dundee, dead by 1644, husband of Janet Geddes, father of Margaret, Elizabeth, Janet, and Marion. [LC#2352][NAS.RS35.S2.III.321, etc]

**GOURLAY, JAMES,** born 1604, a maltman burgess, died 4 July 1648. [Howff]

**GOURLAY, JOHN,** town councillor of Dundee, 1685. [RPCS.XI.62]

**GOURLAY, MARGARET,** daughter of Walter Gourlay a maltman in Dundee, and spouse of Thomas Fyffe a baker in Dundee, 1631. [NAS.RS35.S1.VIII.168]

**GOURLAY, PATRICK,** born 1620, town clerk of Dundee, died 16 December 1667. [Howff]

**GOURLAY, WALTER,** born 1582, a maltman burgess, died 28 April 1628. [Howff]

**GRAHAM, MARGARET,** daughter of James Graham a merchant in Dundee, and spouse of David Ramsay a merchant in Arbroath, 1684. [NAS.RD35.S3.VIII.43]

**GRAINGER, MARGARET,** spouse of George Gardyne a merchant in Dundee, 1684. [NAS.RS35.S3.VIII.50]

**GRAY, ALEXANDER,** the elder, a baxter burgess, died 5 August 1613, husband of Elspet Smythe. [Howff]

**GRAY, ALEXANDER,** in Dundee, 1614. [DSL]

**GRAY, ANDREW,** of Longlogie, Dundee, 1680. [NAS.AC7/5]

**GRAY, CHRISTIAN,** relict of Thomas Steill a maltman in Dundee, 1688. [NAS.RD4.63.279]

**GRAY, DAVID,** a bonnetmaker in the Hill of Dundee, husband of Elspeth Butter, 1631. [NAS.RS35.S1.VIII.183]

**GRAY, JACK,** from Dundee, settled in Newhaven, Rotterdam, married Bessie Jones from Dysart, in Rotterdam in 1619. [Rotterdam Marriage Register]

**GRAY, JAMES,** a burgess of Dundee, 1612. [RPCS.IX.50]

**GRAY, JAMES,** a brabiner burgess of Dundee, husband of Isobel Spankie who died 26 April 1625, testament, Comm. Edinburgh, 1626. [Howff]

**GRAY, JAMES,** of Bullion, 1680. [NAS.AC7/5]

**GRAY, JOHN,** a maltman, Comm. Edinburgh, 1609, [NAS]; wife Margaret Hill, born 1554, died 20 October 1630. [Howff]

**GRAY, JOHN,** a sailor in Dundee, husband of Agnes Kirkcaldy, 1643. [NAS.RS35.S2.II.394]

**GRAY, JOHN,** in Foulis, heir to his father John Gray skinner burgess of Dundee, 1633. [NAS.S/H]

**GRAY, JOHN,** a hammerman, husband of Alison More, born 1599, died 10 November 1669. [Howff]

**GRAY, JOHN,** husband of Janet Hill born 165-, died 16 August 168-. [Howff]

**GRAY, JOHN,** a merchant in Dundee, dead by 1680, father of Andrew and James. [NAS.AC7/5]

**GRAY, PATRICK,** in Dundee, 1612. [RPCS.IX.385]

**GRAY, PATRICK,** a mariner burgess of Dundee, husband of Anna, daughter of Michael Ramsay in North Ferry, 1679. [NAS.RS35.S3.VII.376]

**GRAY, RICHARD,** merchant in Dundee, 1661, [NAS.RD4.3.484]; master of the packhouse and weighhouse of Dundee, 1684. [NAS.AC7/6]

**GRAY, ROBERT,** a mariner of Dundee, relict Anna Gray, 1680. [NAS.RS35.S3.VII.376]

**GRAY, THOMAS,** master of the Marie of Dundee, 1676. [NAS.AC7.4]

**GRAY, THOMAS,** a merchant burgess of Dundee, husband of Euphan Rollo died, aged 64, in 16... [Howff]

**GRAY, WILLIAM,** born 1580, sheriff clerk of Forfar, died 19 April 1629, husband of Marion Doig. [Howff]

**GRAY, WILLIAM,** a mariner in Dundee, 1680, 1688. [NAS.AC7/5; RD3.68.414]

**GRIEVE, GEORGE,** an apothecary in Dundee, husband of Margaret Davidson, 1685. [NAS.RS35.S3.VIII.168]

**GUILD, BESSIE,** spouse of John Dewar a weaver on the Hill of Dundee, 1666. [NAS.RS35.S3.III.237]

**GUILD, CHRISTINA,** relict of Andrew Jack a baker in Dundee, 1649. [NAS.RS35.S2.III.237]

**GUTHRIE, ALEXANDER,** born 1569, a maltman burgess, died 14 May 1611, husband of Elspet Taylor. [Howff]

**GUTHRIE, GILBERT,** a merchant in Dundee, husband of Jean Guthrie, 1652. [NAS.RS35.S2.IV.4, etc]

**GUTHRIE, HENRY,** a merchant burgess of Dundee, died 29 November 1635, husband of (1) Barbara Baldovie, born 1572, died March 1624, (2) Myrable Gardyne, testaments, 1626, 1632, 1636, Comm. Brechin. [NAS] [Howff]

**GUTHRIE, HENRY,** a merchant in Dundee, formerly a student of divinity, son of William Guthrie a bailie of Dundee, 1676. [NAS.RS35.S3.VI.434]

**GUTHRIE, HENRY,** from Dundee to Maryland in 1699. [NAS.AC8/12]

**GUTHRIE, JAMES,** born in Dundee on 20 April 1669, son of Reverend John Guthrie and his wife Isabel Lamb(died 1683), a merchant in Stockholm, husband of Christian Scott, died 1 April 1710. [F.5.320][Howff]

**GUTHRIE, JOHN,** merchant burgess of Dundee, husband of Margaret Lessells born ca.1575, died 7 May 1625, parents of William. [Howff]; testaments, 1625/1628, Comm. Brechin. [NAS]

**GUTHRIE, JOHN,** a merchant burgess of Dundee, husband of Helen Dinnes, 16…(?) [Howff]

**GUTHRIE, JOHN,** born 13 August 1631, son of Reverend James Guthrie in Arbirlot, minister of the Second Charge from 1667 to 1685. Husband of Isabel Lamb, parents of John, Isobel, James, Nicolas, Robert, Ann, and Alexander. [F.5.320][NAS.RS35.S3.VI.218]

**GUTHRIE, PATRICK,** the elder, merchant burgess, born 1557, died 23 September 1625, husband of Margaret Wilkieson, testament, 16 January 1626, Comm. Brechin. [Howff]

**GUTHRIE, PATRICK,** born 1608, a merchant burgess of Dundee, died 10 August 1674, husband of Christian Wright born 1609, died 1 April 1661, testament, 1662, Comm. Brechin. [NAS][Howff]

**GUTHRIE, WILLIAM,** a merchant in Dundee, father of Gilbert, Henry, husband of Margaret Lyon, 1688. [NAS.RD3.69.555]

**HALIBURTON, ALEXANDER,** 1614. [DSL]

**HALIBURTON, ALEXANDER,** of Balgillo, a merchant and former bailie of Dundee, husband of Margaret Hunter, 1631. [NAS.RS35.S1.VIII.71]

**HALIBURTON, JANET,** spouse of James Ostler, brother of John Ostler a brabiner in the Hill of Dundee, 1654. [NAS.RS35.S2.IV.333]

**HALIBURTON, ROBERT,** master of the Thomas of Dundee, 1614. [DSL]

**HALIBURTON, THOMAS,** piermaster of Dundee, 1612. [DSL]

**HALIBURTON, T.,** a bailie of Dundee, 1614. [DSL]

**HALIBURTON, THOMAS,** dean of guild of Dundee, 1644.
[LC#2352]
**HALIBURTON, THOMAS,** born 1662, son of A. Haliburton and IM, died in January 1672. [Howff]
**HALIBURTON, WILLIAM,** master of the Patience of Dundee, 1613.
[DSL]
**HALIBURTON, WILLIAM,** a skipper from Dundee, 1642.
[GAR.ONA.86.258.481]
**HALS, WILLIAM,** a seaman from Dundee, in Dutch service, 1634.
[GAR.ONA.194.205.302]
**HAMILTON, ANNA,** only daughter of John Hamilton of Machlinhoill, spouse to Robert Acheson of Sydserff, heir to her grandfather Robert Hamilton a merchant burgess of Dundee, 1653. [NAS.S/H]; also heir to her father's brother Robert Hamilton, son of Robert Hamilton a burgess of Dundee, 1653. [NAS.S/H]; also to her father John Hamilton of Mauchlinhoill, 1653. [NAS.S/H]
**HASEWELL, JOHN,** a mariner in Dundee, husband of Margaret, daughter of John Myles, 1667. [NAS.RS35.S3.III.285, etc]
**HAY, JAMES,** master of the Lyoness of Dundee, 1614. [DSL]
**HAY, WILLIAM,** a weaver in Dundee, husband of Marion Steven, 1644. [NAS.RS35.S2.II.538, etc]
**HEICH, WILLIAM,** a notary in Dundee, 1621. [RGS.VIII.799]
**HENDERSON, ANDREW,** uncle of George Henderson, in Dundee, 1643. [NAS.RS35.S2.II.530]
**HENDERSON, ELSPETH,** relict of Robert Gilzeat a sailor in Dundee, 1649. [NAS.RS35.S2.III.462]
**HENDERSON, ISABEL,** relict of John Scrymgeour a merchant in Dundee, 1653. [NAS.RS35.S2.IV.132]
**HENDERSON, PATRICK,** a glazier burgess in Dundee, husband of Catherine Man who died 17 September 1677. [Howff]
**HERIOT, JANET,** spouse of Andrew Walker a tailor in Dundee, 1649. [NAS.RS35.S2.III.493]
**HERON, ROBERT,** a bonnet-maker burgess of Dundee, husband of Isobel Spens, born 1618, died 7 September 1642. [Howff]
**HERRIES, ISABEL,** spouse of Thomas Man a merchant in Dundee, 1661. [NAS.RS35.S3.I.363]
**HILL, ANDREW,** a baker in Dundee, 1620. [NAS.RS35.S1.I.171]
**HILL, ISOBEL,** mother of William Smith a weaver in Hilltown, Dundee, 1692. [NAS.RS35.S3.IX.532]

HILL, JOHN, husband of Euphemia Gray, born 1666, died 20 June 1695. [Howff]
HODGE, JAMES, a skinner in Dundee, 1611. [RPCS.IX.197]
HODGE, JOHN, a bonnet-maker, and his wife Jeillis Bennet in Dundee, 1612. [RPCS.IX.385]
HODGE, JOHN, a skipper in Dundee, father of Margaret, 1661. [NAS.RD3.3.169]
HODGE, PATRICK, a cordiner in Dundee, 1612. [RPCS.IX.385]
HOG, JAMES, a bonnetmaker on the Hill of Dundee, husband of Elizabeth, daughter of James Richardson there, 1660. [NAS.RS35.S3.I.35]
HOOD, JOHN, a gardener in Dudhope then on the Hill of Dundee, husband of Agnes Quarrier, 1676. [NAS.RS35.S3.VI.238]
HOWATT, JOHN, a maltman in Dundee, husband of Christian Shewan, 1654. [NAS.RS35.S2.IV.403]
HOWIE, ROBERT, minister of St Mary's, 1598-1605. [F.5.315]
HUNTER, JAMES, in 1612. [WCB#186]
HUNTER, PATRICK, a glazier burgess in Dundee, husband of Catherine Man who died 17 September 1677. [Howff]
JACK, ALEXANDER, husband of Anna Smith, in Hill of Dundee, 1692. [NAS.RS35.S3.IX.134]
JACK, ALEXANDER, a maltman in Dundee, husband of Eupham Weir, 1632. [NAS.RS35.S1.VIII.260; S2.I.50]
JACK, BARBARA, spouse of John Corbet a sailor in Dundee, 1631. [NAS.RS35.S1.VIII.19]
JACK, ELSPETH, spouse of Alexander Jackson a merchant in Dundee, 1648. [NAS.RS35.S2.III.264]
JACK, JAMES, born 1568, a skipper burgess of Dundee, died 28 May 1611, husband of Margaret Baldovie, testaments, 1612/1624, Comm. Brechin. [NAS][Howff]
JACK, JANET, spouse of John Bathgate a notary public in Dundee, 1631. [NAS.RS35.S1.VIII.260]
JACK, JOHN, born 1548, a mason burgess of Dundee, husband of Janet Essie, born 1558, parents of John, born 1578, all died on 15 August 1608. [Howff]
JACK, MARGARET, daughter of William Jack a burgess of Dundee, 1668. [NAS.RS35.S3.IV.121]
JACK, MARJORIE, spouse of James Beattie postmaster and stabler in Dundee, 1653. [NAS.RS35.S2.IV.440]

**JACK, MARION,** spouse of James Robertson a merchant and weaver in the Hill of Dundee, 1684. [NAS.RS35.S3.VIII.90]

**JACK, PATRICK,** a merchant in Dundee, 1637. [NAS.RS35.S2.I.65]

**JACK, ROBERT,** a merchant in Dundee, husband of Agnes Wemyss, 1631. [NAS.RS35.S1.VIII.260]

**JACK, THOMAS,** a merchant burgess of Dundee, 1621. [LC#1891]

**JACK, THOMAS,** fiar of Woodhill, merchant in Dundee, relict Janet Wichton, 1638. [NAS.RS35.S2.I.177]

**JACKSON, ALEXANDER,** a merchant in Dundee, husband of Elspeth Jack, 1648. [NAS.RS35.S2.III.264]

**JACKSON, GILBERT,** portioner of Peatie, merchant in Dundee, 1661. [NAS.RS35.S3.I.204]

**JACKSON, JOHN,** the elder, at Hobert's Milne on the Dichty, burgess of Dundee, 1638. [NAS.RS35.S2.I.489]

**JACKSON, PATRICK,** a merchant in Dundee, husband of Christian Brown, 1666; born 1610, a maltman burgess, died in May 1668, husband of Margaret Jackson, testament, 1667, Comm. Brechin. [NAS][Howff][NAS.RS35.S3.III.289]

**JACKSON, PATRICK,** born 1650, died 31 March 1689, husband of Margaret Garden. [Howff]

**JACKSON, WILLIAM,** a maltman in Dundee, 1652. [NAS.RS35.S2.IV.4]

**JARDEN, DONALD,** a maltman in Dundee, husband of Margaret Jack, 1668. [NAS.RS35.S3.IV.121]

**JOBSON, JEAN,** daughter of James Jobson, and spouse of William Constable a flesher in Dundee, 1637. [NAS.RS35.S2.I.40]

**JOHNSON, PETER,** from Dundee, a burgess of Bergen, Norway, in 1625. [SAB]

**JOHNSON, THOMAS,** from Dundee, a burgess of Bergen, Norway, in 1632. [SAB]

**JOHNSTONE, ANDREW,** a merchant from Dundee, was admitted as a citizen of Cracow, Poland, in 1602. [SIP#49]

**JOHNSTONE, SAMUEL,** born 1655, minister of St Mary's from 1699 to 1731, died 24 February 1731. Husband of Isobel Hall, parents of Samuel, Elizabeth, Nathaniel, Joseph and Gabriel. [F.5.316]

**JOHNSTON, WILLIAM,** born 1569, a cordiner burgess, died 2 January 1632. [Howff]

**KEIR, JAMES,** in Argyll's Gait, Dundee, 1611. [RGS.VI.464]

**KEIR, JOHN,** nephew of John Peirson, a skipper in Dundee, 1676. [NAS.RS35.S3.VI.98]

**KEIR, JOHN,** a skipper in Dundee, 1685. [NAS.RS35.S3.VIII.124]

**KEIR, JOHN,** son of John Keir, a skipper in Dundee, formerly in Middelburg, Holland, 1685. [NAS.RS35.S3.VIII.124]

**KELMAN, ALEXANDER,** 1613. [WCB#189]

**KERR, ROBERT,** of Labothie, a merchant in Dundee, husband of Anna Lundie, 1675. [NAS.RS35.S3.VI.94]

**KERR, THOMAS,** a tailor in Dundee, 1601. [RGS.VI.1219]

**KERR, WILLIAM,** a burgess of Dundee, 1649. [NAS.RS35.S2.III.517]

**KEY, DAVID,** a tailor in Dundee, husband of Elizabeth Smith, 1666. [NAS.RS35.S3.III.300]

**KEY, ELSPETH,** daughter of David Key a tailor in Dundee, 1666. [NAS.RS35.S3.III.275]

**KEY, THOMAS,** in Rottenraw or the Hill of Dundee, 1638. [NAS.RS35.S2.I.488]

**KIDD, ALEXANDER,** heir to his father Thomas Kidd in Dundee, 1604. [NAS.S/H]

**KIDD, ALEXANDER,** a merchant in Dundee, 1637. [NAS.RS35.S2.I.65]

**KIDD, ARCHIBALD,** a merchant in Dundee, 1637. [NAS.RS35.S2.I.67]

**KIDD, JAMES,** a burgess of Dundee, heir to his grandfather Archibald Kidd a burgess of Dundee, 1621. [NAS.S/H]

**KIDD, PATRICK,** of Craigie, 1666. [RGS.XI.934]

**KIDD, THOMAS,** son of Andrew Kidd a tailor in Dundee and his wife Helen Brydie, a traveller in Ystad, Denmark, 1612. [DA.CBIII.124]

**KIDD, WILLIAM,** born in Dundee during 1654, son of John Kidd a seaman and Bessie Butchart, a master mariner who settled in New York by 1688, later executed in London for piracy. [NA.HCA.Vol.81; Jackson & Jacobs v. Noell, 1695]

**KINLOCH, DAVID,** born 1559, royal physician, died 1617. [Howff]

**KINLOCH, GEORGE,** master of the Blessing of Dundee, 1614. [DSL]

**KINLOCH, JOHN,** a merchant in Dundee, husband of Christine Dunmuir, 1656. [NAS.RS35.S2.V.151, etc]

**KINLOCH, PATRICK,** a merchant in Dundee and co-owner of the James of Dundee, 1692. [NAS.AC7/9]

**KINLOCH, PETER,** born 1590, a merchant burgess of Dundee, died 27 October 1641, testament, 1643, Comm. Brechin. [NAS][Howff]

**KINLOCH, Mr ROBERT,** schoolmaster of Dundee Grammar School, was admitted as a burgess of Dundee on 21 December 1667. [DBR]

**KINLOCH, WILLIAM,** in Dundee, 1600, a merchant burgess of Dundee, 1612. [RGS.VI.1032][DSL]

**KINLOCH, WILLIAM,** 1609, master of the William of Dundee, 1612. [RGS.VI.148][DSL]

**KINNAIRD, CHRISTIAN,** spouse to Patrick Lin a merchant burgess of Dundee, testament, 27 August 1593, Comm. St Andrews. [NAS]

**KINNAIRD, PATRICK,** born 1586, a mariner, died 18 January 1628, husband of Marjory Gleig. [Howff]

**KINNAIRD, PETER,** a maltman in Dundee, husband of Isobel Gray, 1645. [NAS.RS35.S2.II.505]

**KINNAIRD, WILLIAM,** master of the Hope for Grace of Dundee, 1614. [DSL]

**KINNEMONT, JOHN,** emigrated, with his wife Ann and children Patrick and John, to Maryland in 1654, was granted 400 acres in Talbot County on 16 August 1680 which he named Dundee. [MSA: LOR]

**KINNERIS, ANDREW,** in Cowgait, Dundee, 1600, 1612. [RGS.VI.1060][DSL]

**KINNERIS, ANDREW,** a skipper in Dundee, 1644. [NAS.RS35.S2.I.413]

**KINNERIS, JAMES,** a skipper in Dundee, husband of Christina Fleming, 1640. [NAS.RS35.S2.I.413]

**KINNERIS, WILLIAM,** a merchant burgess of Dundee, 1612. [DSL]

**KINNERIS, WILLIAM,** master of the Hope for Grace of Dundee, 1612, 1614. [DSL]

**KIRKLAND, JOHN,** town councillor of Dundee, 1685. [RPCS.XI.62]

**KNIGHT, GEORGE,** master of the James of Dundee, 1612; master of the Jonas of Dundee, 1614. [DSL]

**KNIGHT, GILBERT,** a skipper burgess of Dundee, husband of Alison Constable in the Ferry, born 1583, died in May 1623, testament, 1624, Comm. Brechin. [NAS][Howff]

**KNIGHT, GILBERT,** a burgess of Dundee, 1638. [NAS.RS35.S2.I.182]

**KNIGHT, HENRY,** a skipper in Dundee, 1638. [NAS.RS35.S2.I.182]
**KNIGHT, WILLIAM,** son of Gilbert Knight, a skipper in Dundee, 1638. [NAS.RS35.S2.I.182]
**KYD, ISOBEL,** in Dundee, spouse of William Knight, testament, Comm. St Andrews, 1607. [NAS]; resident of St Margaret's Close, Dundee, 1612. [WCB#187]
**KYD, J.,** kirkmaster of Dundee, 1614. [DSL]
**KYD, PATRICK,** a bailie of Dundee, 1614. [DSL]
**KYD, PATRICK,** a merchant in Dundee, 1699. [NAS.RD4/84/71, etc]
**KYD, ROBERT,** a baxter burgess of Dundee, testament, Comm. St Andrews, 1591. [NAS]
**KYD, WILLIAM,** a weaver on the Hill of Dundee, husband of Janet Pyrot, 1661. [NAS.RS35.S3.I.216]
**KYLE, JAMES,** a surgeon burgess of Dundee, husband of (1) Marjory ....., born 1608, died in June 1638, (2) Margaret Rankin, testaments, 1642, 1663, Comm. Brechin. [NAS]
**KYLE, THOMAS,** born 1567, a mariner and merchant burgess of Dundee, died in 1623, husband of Marion Guidlet, testament, 1624, Comm. Brechin. [NAS]
**KYNNEIR, JOHN,** and his wife Eupham Gray born 1568, died 1 March 1627. [Howff]
**LAMB, CHRISTIAN,** sometime spouse to Walter Jobson a maltman burgess of Dundee, Comm.St Andrews, 1599. [NAS]
**LAMB, WILLIAM,** a weaver on the Hill of Dundee, 1667, husband of (1) Janet Smith, (2) Matilda Smith. [NAS.RS35.S3.III.303]
**LAUDER, ROBERT,** a writer in Dundee, husband of Euphan Bathgate, 1673. [NAS.RS35.S3.V.334]
**LAWSON, DAVID,** son of John Lawson a merchant in Dundee, settled in Naumsburg, Prussia, by 1616. [DA, birthbrief, 22.8.1616]
**LAWSON, JAMES,** a baxter in Dundee, 1680. [NAS.AC7/5]
**LAWSON, JOHN,** jr., burgess and deacon of the baxters, died 3 April 16-6, aged 34, husband of Christian Mitchell. [Howff]
**LAWSON, PATRICK,** a tailor burgess of Dundee, husband of Margaret Tyrie, 1656. [LC#2496]
**LEES, JAMES,** in Dundee, 1684. [NAS.AC7/6]
**LEES, WILLIAM,** from Dundee, a seaman in Portuguese service, 1641. [GAR.ONA.202.142.185]
**LENNOX, JOHN,** of Geddehall, a messenger in Dundee, husband of Elizabeth Simpson, 1675. [NAS.RS35.S3.VI.176, etc]

**LEONARD, GILBERT,** a cooper in Dundee, 1670.
[NAS.RS35.S3.IV.287]

**LESLIE, ROBERT,** a merchant in Dundee, 1667.
[NAS.RS35.S3.III.258]

**LESLIE, WILLIAM,** a merchant in Dundee, husband of Margaret Anderson, parents of James, 1686. [NAS.RS35.S3.VIII.365]

**LESSILLIS, JAMES,** a maltman in Dundee, 1645.
[NAS.RS35.S2.II.538]

**LEYIS, WILLIAM,** a merchant in Dundee, husband of Christian, daughter of George Watt a sailor there, 1639.
[NAS.RS35.S2.I.510/2]

**LINDSAY, ANNE,** from Dundee, married James Grant, a soldier from Elgin, in Schiedam, the Netherlands, on 19 December 1637. [Schiedam Marriage Register]

**LINDSAY, DAVID,** minister of St Mary's, 1606 to 1619, then Bishop of Brechin. [F.5.315]

**LINDSAY, DAVID,** a mason in Dundee, 1685.
[NAS.RS35.S3.VIII.271]

**LINDSAY, JAMES,** master of the Swan of Dundee, 1614. [DSL]

**LINDSAY, JAMES,** a skipper of Dundee, in Gothenburg, 1642.
[NAS.RS35.S2.II.57]

**LINDSAY, JANET,** sometime spouse to Henry Clerk a cordiner burgess of Dundee, Comm. St Andrews, 1606. [NAS]

**LINDSAY, MARGARET,** sometime spouse of John Wedderburn a skipper burgess of Dundee, testament, Comm. St Andrews, 1600.
[NAS]

**LINDSAY, Major ROBERT,** a burgess of Dundee, husband of Margaret Milne, parents of Alexander and Robert, 1653.
[NAS.RS35.S2.IV.230]

**LINDSAY, ROBERT,** a merchant in Dundee, co-owner of the Marie of Dundee, 1676. [NAS.AC7.4]

**LINDSAY, THOMAS,** a goldsmith and burgess of Dundee, 1612.
[RPCS.IX.50]

**LINDSAY, THOMAS,** a goldsmith, was admitted as a burgess of Dundee on 6 March 1662; Deacon of the Hammerman Incorporation of Dundee in 1668. [DBR][DA.GD.HF.HI]

**LINDSAY, THOMAS,** a baxter in Dundee, father of Christian, 1653.
[NAS.RS35.S2.IV.80]

**LINDSAY, WILLIAM,** master of the Magdalene of Dundee, 1614.
[DSL]

**LOCHMALONY, GEORGE,** a skipper in Dundee, father of Euphan, spouse of Robert Stirling a merchant there, and Margaret, spouse of Andrew Bathgate merchant and treasurer of Dundee, 1668. [NAS.RS35.RS35.S3.III.445]

**LOCHMALONY, WILLIAM,** father of George a skipper in Dundee, 1668. [NAS.RS35.S3.III.445

**LOVELL, ELSPET,** sometime spouse to Andrew Watson, in Dundee, testament, Comm. St Andrews, 1588. [NAS]

**LOVELL, ELSPET,** relict of Robert Wedderburn the younger sometime a burgess of Dundee, testament, Comm. St Andrews, 1598. [NAS]

**LOVELL, MARIOTA,** heir to her brother James Lovell in the lands of West Ferry, 1607. [Retours]

**LOVELL, SYBILLA,** heir to her brother James Lovell in the lands of West Ferry, 1607. [Retours]

**LOW, JAMES,** a burgess of Dundee, 1612. [RPCS.IX.50]

**LUGGATT, JOHN,** born ca.1642, a slater in Dundee, died 1709, husband of A.N., testament 1709, Comm. Brechin. [NAS] [Howff]

**LUGTON, ANDREW,** a merchant in Dundee, 1613. [DSL]

**LYCHTOUN, CHRISTAIN,** in 1613. [WCB#185]

**LYELL, WILLIAM,** in Dundee, 1656. [LC#2496]

**LYELL, WILLIAM,** a clothier on the Hill of Dundee, 1692. [NAS.RS35.S3.IX.46]

**LYN, FERGUS,** a litster in Dundee, 1638. [NAS.RS35.S2.I.128]

**LYN, PATRICK,** in Dundee, 1612. [RPCS.IX.385]

**LYN, ROBERT,** a litster in Dundee, father of Bessie, Isabel, Janet and Christian, 1649. [NAS.RS35.S2.III.381]

**LYON, JAMES,** a merchant in Dundee, 1692. [NAS.AC7/9; RS35.S3.VII.339]

**LYON, JOHN,** a skinner burgess of Dundee, husband of Matilda Peirson who died 14 February 1628. [Howff]

**LYON, PATRICK,** a burgess of Dundee, 1644. [NAS.RS35.S2.II.428]

**LYON, THOMAS,** a hammerman burgess of Dundee, testament, 29 March 1599, Comm. St Andrews. [NAS]

**MCULLO, THOMAS,** a merchant in Dundee, husband of Isabella Davidson, 1621. [LC#1891]

**MCDUFF, GILBERT,** 1612. [WCB#187]

**MCINTOSH or MCKENE, ALESTAIR,** a maltman in Dundee, 1637. [NAS.RS35.S2.I.48]

**MCKENE, or TOSCH, ALASTAIR,** father of Thomas, a maltman in Dundee, 1656. [NAS.RS35.S2.V.276]

**MCLEAN, JOHN,** born 1621, merchant burgess, died 10 January 1696, husband of Agnes Forrester, testament, 1666, Comm. Brechin. [NAS][Howff]

**MCMILLAR, FERGUS,** a merchant burgess of Dundee, testament, Comm. St Andrews, 1594. [NAS]

**MACHAN, DAVID,** born 1596, skipper in the Ferry, died October 1632, husband of Jean Watson, testament, 1633, Comm. Brechin. [NAS][Howff]

**MACHIN, DAVID,** a merchant burgess of Dundee, 1678. [NAS.AC7.4]

**MACHAN, JEAN,** daughter of John Machan a skipper in North Ferry of Tay, relict of (1) William Duncan skipper in Dundee, and (2) Michael Ramsay in the North Ferry of Tay, 1648. [NAS.RS35.S2.III.464]

**MACHAN, JOHN,** in the Ferry, and his spouse Isobel Knight, father of Ann, testament, 1640, Comm. Brechin. [NAS][NAS.RS35.S2.I.182/III.464]

**MACKIE, or MACKIESON, DAVID,** a baxter in Dundee, husband of Christian Ritchie, 1648. [NAS.RS45.S2.III.457]

**MACKIE, ISOBEL,** spouse to James Doig a baxter burgess of Dundee, testament, 24 January 1606, Comm. St Andrews. [NAS]

**MACKIE, or MACKISON, JAMES,** a baxter in Dundee, 1638. [NAS.RS35.S2.I.396]

**MACKIE, or MACKISON, THOMAS,** a burgess of Dundee, husband of Margaret Waterston, 1639.[NAS.RS35.S2.I.396]

**MACKIE, THOMAS,** a crofter in Dundee, 1666. [RGS.XI.883]

**MACKISON, JAMES,** a litster in Dundee, 1679. [NAS.RS35.S3.VII.108]

**MAIDEN, WILLIAM,** a mason burgess of Dundee, husband of Christian Donaldson, born 1610, died 2 April 1654. [Howff]

**MAITLAND, ......,** Collector of Customs at Dundee, 1686. [RPCS.XI.426]

**MAN, DAVID,** a merchant in Dundee, 1612. [RPCS.IX.385]

**MAN, JAMES,** born 1561, a merchant in Dundee, 1612. [DSL], died 13 September 1640, [Howff]; husband of Grissell Clayhills, born 1568, died 1 January 1648. [Howff]

**MAN, JAMES,** a merchant in Dundee, 1678/1679, 1685, 1688. [NAS.AC7.4/5; RD4.62.45][RPCS.XI.62] [NAS.RS35.S3.VI.293]

**MAN, JOHN,** a bailie and merchant in Dundee, 1679, nephew of John Peirson a skipper there, husband of Margaret Scrymgeour, died 1686. [NAS.AC7.5][Howff][NAS.RS35.S3.VI.98]

**MAN, ROBERT,** skinner in Dundee, 1611. [RPCS.IX.197]

**MAN, THOMAS,** a merchant in Dundee, husband of Isabel Herries, 1661. [NAS.RS35.S3.I.363]

**MAN, WILLIAM,** a bailie of Dundee, 1600. RGS.VI.1060]

**MAN, WILLIAM,** a seaman from Dundee in Dutch service, 1634. [GAR.ONA.194.220.323]

**MAN, WILLIAM,** a merchant in Dundee, father of Thomas, 1638. [NAS.RS35.S3.I.210]

**MANFOD, ANDREW,** a merchant skinner in Dundee, husband of Catherine Nicoll, 1643. [NAS.RS35.S2.II.351, etc]

**MARTIN, DAVID,** a clothier on the Hill of Dundee, relict Margaret Drummond, 1644. [NAS.RS35.S2.II.535, etc]

**MARTIN, GEORGE,** born 1615, son of George Martin and his wife Catherine Schevez, minister of the Second Charge from 1658 to 1660, died 21 April 1660. Husband of Barbara Gledstanes, parents of George, James, William, Alexander, Katherine, Helen and Jane. [F.5.319]

**MASON, JOHN,** born 1554, a pynour burgess of Dundee, died 15 February, 1604, testament, 1604, Comm. Edinburgh; relict Janet Thomson, testament, 1613, Comm. Brechin. [NAS][Howff]

**MASTERTON, JOHN,** a flesher in Dundee, son of ..... Masterton and Margaret Lochmalony, 1654, husband of Mary Lyon, 1666. [NAS.RS35.S2.IV.291; S3.III.49]

**MATHESON, ANDREW,** of the bonnetmakers craft of Dundee, 1612. [RPCS.IX.197]

**MATTHEW, HENRY,** a seaman from Dundee, aboard the Dutch ship Seacalf, testament, 23 August 1631. [GAR.ONA.191.243.320]

**MATTHEW, JOHN,** a seaman from Dundee in Dutch service, 1641. [GAR.ONA.201.236.320]

**MATTHEW, THOMAS,** in Hilltown, husband of Janet, daughter of John Shear a fuller, 1666. [NAS.RS35.S3.III.64]

**MATTHEW, THOMAS,** a merchant in Dundee, husband of Janet Wardroper, 1698. [NAS.RS35.S3.X.68]

**MAXWELL, DAVID,** treasurer of Dundee, 1685; a merchant in Dundee, 1699. [RPCS.XI.62][NAS.RD4/84/371, 1091]
**MAXWELL, JOHN,** heir to his father John Maxwell a wright burgess of Dundee, 1626. [NAS.S/H]
**MAXWELL, PATRICK,** a litster in Dundee, father of Barbara, George, Janet, 1686. [NAS.RS35.S3.VIII.366, etc]
**MAXWELL, ROBERT,** a merchant in Dundee, father of Agnes, Barbara, Christian, Euphan, Hugh, and Janet, 1677. [NAS.RS35.S3.VI.360]
**MEALL, JOHN,** born 1570, a maltman burgess of Dundee, died 4 March 1632, husband of Euphemia Dorward, testaments, 1632 and 1635, Comm. Brechin. [NAS][Howff]
**MEARNS, ALEXANDER,** a merchant in Dundee, 1699. [NAS.RD2/82/910, etc]
**MEARNS, THOMAS,** a merchant in Dundee, 1699. [NAS.RD2/82/910, etc]
**MELDRUM, JOHN,** a merchant burgess of Dundee, 1612. [DSL]
**MELVILL, JOHN,** a merchant in Dundee, 1677. [NAS.RS35.S3.VI.287]
**MILL, JOHN,** burgess of Dundee, husband of Helen Kinneris, born 1555, died 1617. [Howff]
**MILLER, THOMAS,** a bonnetmaker on the Hill of Dundee, husband of Janet Young, 1660. [NAS.RS35.S3.I.36, etc]
**MILN, A.,** born 1584, bailie of Dundee, died 1651. [Howff]
**MILNE, ALEXANDER,** son of Alexander Milne, a mealmaker on the Hill of Dundee, 1660. [NAS.RS35.S3.I.131]
**MILNE, ROBERT,** a burgess of Dundee, 1632. [NAS.RS35.S1.VIII.268]
**MILNE, WILLIAM,** a weaver on the Hill of Dundee, 1676. [NAS.RS35.S3.VI.120]
**MINIMAN, JOHN,** born 1559, a merchant burgess in Dundee, died 20 October 1609, husband of (1) Katherine Keir, born 1546, died 1 October 1609, (2) Margaret Bonnar, father of John and Elizabeth, testament, 1609, Comm. Edinburgh. [NAS][Howff] [NAS.RS35.S3.VI.174]
**MITCHELL, ANDREW,** skinner in Dundee, 1611. [RPCS.IX.197]
**MITCHELL, GEORGE,** a maltman in Dundee, 1612. [RPCS.IX.385]
**MITCHELL, GEORGE,** a bonnetmaker on the Hill of Dundee, husband of Jean Young, 1660. [NAS.RS35.S3.I.36]

**MITCHELL, JOHN,** a mariner in Dundee, husband of Isobel Currier, 1682. [NAS.RS35.S3.VII.533]

**MITCHELSON, GILBERT,** a maltman in Dundee, father of Janet, 1695. [NAS.RS35.S3.IX.536]

**MONCUR, GEORGE,** a merchant in Dundee, 1688. [NAS.RD2.69.500]

**MONCUR, JAMES,** master of the Edward, and a merchant burgess of Dundee, 1612; master of the James of Dundee, 1613. [DSL]

**MONTAGO, JOHN,** born 1601, a baxter burgess of Dundee, died 26 December 1647. [Howff]

**MOREIS, ROBERT,** a merchant burgess of Dundee, 1613. [DSL]

**MORGAN, ANDREW,** in Dundee, father of Janet, 1699. [NAS.RS35.S3.X.289]

**MORRISON, ANDREW,** a sailor in Dundee, husband of Catharine Smythe, 1638. [NAS.RS35.S2.I.399]

**MORRISON, ANDREW,** a merchant in Dundee, husband of Agnes Fleming, 1652, 1680, father of Agnes and Margaret. [NAS.AC7/5; RS35.S2.IV.30]

**MORRISON, JAMES,** a litster and merchant in Dundee, father of Andrew, James, and Patrick, 1644. [NAS.RS35.S3.II.314]

**MORTIMER, JANET,** daughter of Andrew Mortimer a burgess of Dundee and his wife Christian Small, settled in Stubbekobing, Denmark, by 1607. [Dundee birthbrief, DA.CB111.69]

**MORTON, ROBERT,** maltman on the Hill of Dundee, husband of Jean Sellar, 1642. [NAS.RS35.S2.II.62]

**MOW, JOHN,** burgess of Dundee, husband of Agnes Jameson born 1584, died 1 July 1631. [Howff]

**MUDIE, ANDREW,** a merchant and treasurer of Dundee, husband of (1)Margaret Lochmalonie, (2) Elizabeth Reid, father of Eupham. [NAS.RS35.S2.III.167, etc]

**MUDIE, JAMES,** a merchant burgess of Dundee, husband of Isobel Macky, 1612, 1613, 1621. [RPCS.IX.385][DSL][Howff][NAS.RS35.S1.I.181]

**MUDIE, JAMES,** a sailor in Dundee, husband of Christina, daughter of James Abercrombie a sailor there, 1631. [NAS.RS35.S1.VIII.66]

**MUDIE, JAMES,** son of Thomas Mudie, a braboner in Dundee, 1644. [NAS.RS35.S2.II.401]

**MUDIE, JANET,** daughter of James Mudie, born 1597, died in September 1612. [Howff]

MUDIE, THOMAS, a merchant in Dundee, 1613. [DSL]
MUDIE, Sir THOMAS, of Kinnettles, provost of Dundee, husband of Christian Fletcher, parents of Jean, 1660. [NAS.RS35.S3.I.73]
MUDIE, THOMAS, a merchant in Dundee, 1676; a bailie in 1685; husband of Agnes Bathgate. [NAS.AC7.4; RS35.S3.VI.435] [RPCS.XI.62]
MUIR, JOHN, a burgess of Dundee, 1637. [NAS.RS35.S2.I.150]
MUIR, JOHN, a seaman from Dundee in Dutch service, 1643. [GAR.ONA.205.3.03]
MURESON, ANDREW, a sailor in Dundee, husband of Catherine, daughter of Alexander Smith a merchant there, 1639. [NAS.RS35.S2.I.399]
MURESON, ANDREW, merchant burgess of Dundee, husband of Margaret Ramsay who died 20 May 1666, testament, 1667, Comm. Edinburgh. [Howff][NAS]
MURESON, ROBERT, born 1605, merchant burgess, died 3 September 1637, husband of Helen Collin, testament 1638, Comm. Brechin. [NAS][Howff]
MURRAY, JAMES, in Dundee, 1614. [DSL]
MYLES, DAVID, a hammerman on the Hill of Dundee, 1698. [NAS.RS35.S3.X.69]
MYLES, HENRY, a skipper in Dundee, 1638. [NAS.RS35.S2.I.128]
MYLES, JOHN, a mariner in Dundee, husband of Janet Peirson, father of William, Elizabeth and Margaret, 1693. [NAS.RS35.S3.IX.174]
MYLNE, ALEXANDER, in 1622. [WCB#185]
MYLNE, ALEXANDER, born circa 1618, son of Alexander Mylne a bailie of Dundee, minister of the Second Charge from 1661 to 1665. Husband of Agnes Fletcher, parnts of Alexander, James, Thomas, George, John, Jean, Margaret, and Janet. [F.5.319]
MYLNE, JOHN, a merchant in Dundee, 1612. [DSL]
MYLNE, THOMAS, born 1629, died 1651, brother of Alexander Mylne minister of Forgan. [Howff]
NEILL, JOHN, a surgeon in Dundee, 1612, 1648. [RPCS.IX.385] [NAS.RS35.S2.III.149]
NEISH, WILLIAM, a burgess of Dundee, 1612. [RPCS.IX.50]
NESS, JOHN, a burgh officer, 1597. [WCB#189]
NEWMAN, JOHN, in Seagait, Dundee, 1611. [RGS.VI.464]
NEWTON, WILLIAM, a litster burgess of Dundee, died 27 September 1608. [Howff]

**NICOLL, ANDREW,** a maltman burgess of Dundee, husband of Catherine Jack born 1575, died 3 January 1626, testament, 1626, Comm. Brechin. [NAS][Howff]

**NICOLL, ALEXANDER,** a baxter in Dundee, husband of Agnes Liddell, 1681. [NAS.RS35.S3.VII.411]

**NICOLL, ANDREW,** a baxter in Dundee, 1681. [NAS.RS35.S3.VII.410]

**NICOLL, GILBERT,** a maltman in Dundee, husband of Marion Kyd, father of Catherine, 1637. [NAS.RS35.S2.I.141]

**NICOLL, JAMES,** son of James Nicoll, a maltman in Dundee, 1656. [NAS,RS35.S2.V.205]

**NICOLL, JOHN,** a flesher in Dundee, son of Thomas Nicoll in Balmirmer, husband of Janet Gourlay, 1680. [NAS.RS35.S3.VII.380]

**NICOLL, JOHN,** deacon convenor of the trades of Dundee, husband of Catherine, daughter of Andrew Wardroper a merchant there, 1687. [NAS.RS35.S3.VIII.490]

**NICOLL, ROBERT,** a merchant in Dundee, 1699. [NAS.RD4/84/1262]

**NICOLL, THOMAS,** born 1620, a tailor burgess of Dundee, died 20 May 1668, husband of (1) Catherine Keil, (2) Elisabeth Ogilvie, testament, 1668, Comm. Brechin. [NAS]

**NICOLL, WILLIAM,** a baxter in Dundee, husband of Janet Jack, 1650. [NAS.RS35.S2.III.491]

**NICOLL, WILLIAM,** a hammerman in Kirkton of Strathmartine, formerly in Dundee, husband of Elizabeth Ruthven, 1684. [NAS.RS35.S3.VIII.91]

**NINIAN, JOHN,** a burgess of Dundee, 1612. [RPCS.IX.50]

**NORIE, DAVID,** heir to his second mother Marjory Carmannow in Dundee, 1628. [NAS.S/H]

**NORIE, ROBERT,** born circa 1647, minister of the Second Charge from 1686 to 1689, died in January 1727. Husband of Isabel Guthrie. [F.5.320][NAS.RS35.S3.IX.464/553]

**OCHTERLONY, JOHN,** in Cowgait, Dundee, 1600. [RGS.VI.1061]

**OGILVIE, GEORGE,** the younger, a maltman in Dundee, 1699. [NAS.RD2/83/630]

**OGILVIE, GILBERT,** skinner burgess of Dundee, 1620. [RGS.VIII.799]

**OGILVY, WILLIAM,** in Dundee, 1614. [DSL]

**OLIPHANT, WILLIAM**, master of the Henry of Dundee, pre 1680. [NAS.AC7/5]

**OSTLER, DAVID**, a mealdealer on the Hill of Dundee, husband of Bessie Paterson, parents of Thomas, 1644. [NAS.RS35.S2.II.485]

**OSTLER, JAMES**, brother of John Ostler, a brabiner on the Hill of Dundee, husband of Janet Halyburton, 1653. [NAS.RS35.S2.IV.173, etc]

**OSTLER, JOHN**, a brabiner on the Hill of Dundee, father of Isabel, 1642. [NAS.RS35.S2.II.61, etc]

**OSTLER, MATTHEW**, a brabiner burgess, husband of Catherine Clark born 1585, died 1616. [Howff]

**OSTLER, MATTHEW**, a weaver on the Hill of Dundee, relict Catherine Coupar, 1639. [NAS.RS35.S2.II.412]

**OSTLER, ROBERT**, husband of Agnes Smith, grandfather of William Ostler, a weaver in Dundee, 1645. [NAS.RS35.S2.II.485]

**OSTLER, WILLIAM**, a weaver on the Hill of Dundee, 1640. [NAS.RS35.S2.I.142]

**OWER, GEORGE**, born 1643, a weaver, died 4 October 1695. [Howff]

**PANTER, ANDREW**, master of the Andrew of Dundee, 1613. [DSL][NAS.RS35.S2.I.150]

**PANTER, PATRICK**, minister of St Mary's, 1626, then professor of Divinity at St Andrews. [F.5.315]

**PARIS, ROBERT**, a cordiner on the Hill of Dundee, father of James a cordiner there, 1656. [NAS.RS35.S2.V.58]

**PATERSON, ANDREW**, a wright-plasterer in Dundee, 1688. [NAS.RD2.69.520]

**PATERSON, JAMES**, a merchant in Dundee, husband of Janet Annand, 1653. [NAS.RS35.S2.IV.100]

**PATERSON, JAMES**, skipper, husband of Agnes Scott born 1616, died 11 November 1669, testament, 1698, Comm. Brechin. [NAS][Howff][NAS.RS35.S3.I.301]

**PATERSON, PETER**, from Dundee, a burgess of Bergen, Norway, in 1635. [SAB]

**PATERSON, THOMAS**, a merchant in Dundee, husband of Ann Cargill, born 1646, died 2 November 1686. [Howff]

**PATTON, JOHN**, a notary in Dundee, 1603, a witness in 1612. [RGS.VI.1482][WCB#187]

**PATULLO, PATRICK,** a merchant in Dundee, 1678. [NAS.AC7.4]
**PATULLO, ROBERT,** skinner burgess of Dundee, husband of Margaret Spens, born 1618, died 15 January 1648. [Howff][NAS.RS35.S2.IV.450]
**PATULLO, WILLIAM,** skinner in Dundee, 1611, 1613. [RPCS.IX.197][DSL]
**PATULLO, WILLIAM,** in Murraygait, Dundee, 1621. [RGS.VIII.1648]
**PAUL, ANDREW,** a maltman burgess of Dundee, dead by 1667, husband of (1) Christian Robertson, dead by 1636, (2) Margaret Brown, born 1616, died 6 October 1645, testament, 1636, 1667, Comm. Brechin. [Howff]
**PAUL, JOHN,** on the Hill of Dundee, son of William Paul, a burgess of Dundee, husband of Rebecca Duff, 1650. [NAS.RS35.S2.III.387]
**PAUL, JOHN,** a maltman in Dundee, husband of (1)Janet Brown, (2) Isobel Spence, 1650. [NAS.RS35.S2.III.388, etc]
**PAUL, THOMAS,** at the East Milne of Baldovan, a maltman in Dundee, 1660. [NAS.RS35.S3.I.72]
**PAUL, THOMAS,** a maltman on the Hill of Dundee, husband of Elizabeth Smith, 1692. [NAS.RS35.S3.IX.39]
**PAUL, WILLIAM,** at the Mylne of Lawbrig, burgess of Dundee, 1643. [NAS.RS35.S2.II.205]
**PEARSON, DAVID,** master of the <u>Margaret of Dundee</u>, 1612, 1614, 1615. [DSL]
**PEARSON, JAMES,** a merchant of Dundee, 1613, 1615. [DSL]
**PEARSON, JAMES,** of Easter Liff, merchant and provost of Dundee, father of Anna, Barbara, Elspeth, Euphan, Janet and Margaret, 1638. [NAS.RS35.S2.I.290, etc]
**PEARSON, JOHN,** a mariner in Dundee, 1656. [NAS.RS35.S2.V.227]
**PEARSON, JOHN,** a merchant in Dundee, 1648. [NAS.RS35.S2.III.145]
**PEARSON, JOHN,** a skipper in Dundee, husband of Margaret Davidson, 1648. [NAS.RS35.S2.III.145]
**PEARSON, THOMAS,** a merchant in Dundee, 1686. [NAS.AC7/7]
**PEEBLES, JOHN,** son of Robert Peebles in Westfield of Dundee, relict Marjorie Young, 1654. [NAS.RS35.S2.IV.418]
**PEEBLES, OLIVER,** a wright, husband of Agnes Culbert, born 1638, died 27 April 1682. [Howff]

**PEIRSON, THOMAS,** born pre 1557, a maltman burgess, died 1607, husband of Magdalene Edeson. [Howff]

**PETRIE, JAMES,** born 1597, a maltman burgess of Dundee, died 5 June 1639, husband of Janet Emeris, father of George, and James, testament, 1640, Comm. Brechin. [NAS][Howff] [NAS.RS35.S2.II.66]

**PETRIE, JAMES,** a merchant in Dundee, 1688. [NAS.RD3.68.661]

**PETRIE, JOHN,** a baxter burgess, husband of Isobel Duncan born 1598, died 13 February 1648. [Howff]

**PETRIE, ROBERT,** born 1574, a maltman burgess, died 11 September 1616. [Howff]

**PHILP, JAMES,** a hammerman in Dundee, husband of Euphan Anderson, 1680. [NAS.RS35.S3.VII.279]

**PHILP, PETER,** a merchant and Customs-waiter in Dundee, 1697. [NAS.RD4.80.421]

**PHILP, ROBERT,** a bonnetmaker on the Hill of Dundee, 1680. [NAS.RS35.VII.279]

**PILMOR, ALEXANDER,** a writer in Dundee, son of James Pilmor clerk depute thereof, 1679. [NAS.RS35.S3.VII.232]

**PILMOR, JAMES,** clerk depute of Dundee and notary in Cupar Angus, 1673. [NAS.RS35.S3.V.192]

**PILMOR, JOHN,** a merchant in Dundee, 1672,1676. [NAS.AC7.4; RS35.S3.V.2]

**PILMURE, ROBERT,** from Dundee, a merchant in Stockholm, testament, 1709. [NAS.CC8.8.84/324]

**PIPER, JOHN,** in Cowgait, Dundee, 1611. [RGS.VI.464]

**PITTILLOCH, ALEXANDER,** a merchant in Dundee, 1676. [NAS.AC7.4]

**PLENDERLEITH, ANDREW,** father of Mariote and John, in Dundee, 1600, 1609. [RGS.VI.1032; VII.148]

**POWRIE, JAMES,** born 1639, a maltman burgess, died 22 January 1698, husband of Alison Liddell, testament, 1686, Comm. Brechin. [NAS][Howff]

**POWRIE, WILLIAM,** a merchant in Dundee, 1613. [DSL]

**QUARRIER, JAMES,** on the Hill of Dundee, 1648. [NAS.RS35.S2.III.2]

**QUARRIER, JAMES,** son of Thomas Quarrier on the Hill of Dundee, 1653. [NAS.RS35.S2.IV.200]

**QUARRIER, JOHN,** a clothier on the Hill of Dundee, husband of Isabel Peter, father of Patrick, 1640. [NAS.RS35.RS2.I.505]

**QUARRIER, THOMAS,** a gardener in Dudhope then on the Hill of Dundee, 1653. [NAS.RS35.S2.IV.200]

**RAE, WILLIAM,** a surgeon on the Hill of Dundee, husband of Elspeth Neilson, father of William, 1638. [NAS.RS35.S2.I.394]

**RAITT, ALEXANDER,** a merchant in Dundee, 1679. [NAS.AC7/5]

**RAITT, JOHN,** a mariner in Dundee, husband of Catharine Crichton, 1699. [NAS.RS35.S3.X.272]

**RAIT, WILLIAM,** born 1617, a bailie and merchant burgess, died 13 December 1674, husband of (1) Christian Mill, (2) Euphan Coupar, testament, 1664, Comm. Brechin. [Howff][NAS] [NAS.RS35.S3.VII.482]

**RAMSAY, ALEXANDER,** of Dundee Grammar School, 1688. [NAS.RD3.69.500]

**RAMSAY, DAVID,** a merchant in Dundee, 1612. [DSL]

**RAMSAY, DAVID,** a maltman, died 2 January 1632, husband of Grisell Watson. [Howff]

**RAMSAY, DAVID,** master of the Black Cock of Dundee, 1678; master of the Andrew of Dundee, 1680; 1691. [NAS.AC7/4; AC7/5; RD2/82/135]

**RAMSAY, DAVID,** a merchant in Dundee, 1699. [NAS.RD3/91/81]

**RAMSAY, GEORGE,** born 1650, a slater burgess of Dundee, died 17 March 1718. [Howff]

**RAMSAY, JAMES,** born 1564, a maltman burgess of Dundee, 1612; died 18 February 1623. [RPCS.IX.50][DSL][Howff]

**RAMSAY, JAMES,** clerk depute of Dundee, 1699. [NAS.RD4/84/1346; RD4/85/991]

**RAMSAY, JAMES,** a slater in Dundee, husband of Margaret Mudie, 1699. [NAS.RS35.S3.X.225]

**RAMSAY, JOHN,** skinner in Dundee, 1611, 1621. [RPCS.IX.197] [LC#1891]

**RAMSAY, JOHN,** treasurer of Dundee, 1622. [WCB#185][NAS.RS35.S2.I.157]

**RAMSAY, JOHN,** a sailor in Dundee, husband of Isobel Knight, 1648. [NAS.RS35.S2.III.65]

**RAMSAY, MICHAEL,** in North Ferry of Dundee, husband of Jean Machan, 1648. [NAS.RS35.S2.III.65]

**RAMSAY, ROBERT,** a merchant in Dundee, 1676. [NAS.AC7.4]

**RAMSAY, WALTER,** a sailor in Dundee, 1644. [NAS.RS35.S2.II.409]

**RAMSAY, WILLIAM,** master of the bark Fortune of Dundee, 1612.
[DSL]
**RAMSAY, WILLIAM,** born 1570, a merchant burgess of Dundee, died 2 February 1640, father of Grisell, husband of Margaret Bellie, born 1575, died 2 March 1629. [Howff]
**RANKIN, ALEXANDER,** in Dundee, 1614. [DSL]
**RANKIN, ANDREW,** master of the David of Dundee, 1614. [DSL]
**RANKIN, ROBERT,** master of the James of Dundee, 1692. [NAS.AC7/9]
**RANKIN, WALTER,** a merchant burgess of Dundee, 1612. [DSL]
**RANKIN, WALTER,** master of the Christian of Dundee, 1627. [NAS.AC7.2.13]
**REID, ALEXANDER,** a bailie of Dundee, 1697. [NAS.RS35.S3.IX.542]
**REID, WILLIAM,** a merchant in Dundee, 1693. [NAS.RS35.S3.IX.349]
**RHIND, ALEXANDER,** born 1555, a timmerman burges of Dundee, died 10 May 1630, husband of Margaret Maxwell. [Howff]
**RHIND, ALEXANDER,** a merchant burgess of Dundee, husband of Barbara Guthrie, testament, 1626, Comm. Brechin. [NAS][Howff]
**RICHARDSON, JAMES,** a bonnetmaker on the Hill of Dundee, relict Jean Langlands, father of Elizabeth and Margaret, 1660. [NAS.RS35.S3.I.35]
**RICHIE, WILLIAM,** clerk of the Magdalene of Dundee, 1614. [DSL]
**RITCHIE, THOMAS,** in the Hill of Dundee, 1684. [NAS.RS35.S3.VIII.69]
**ROB, or ROBERTSON, PATRICK,** a cordiner burgess of Dundee, husband of Bessie Wrighht born 1626, died 25 January 1670, testament, 1670, Comm. Brechin. [NAS][Howff]
**ROBERTSON, ALEXANDER,** a merchant in Dundee, husband of Anna Oliphant, 1698. [NAS.RS35.S3.X.297]
**ROBERTSON, DAVID,** born 1536, died 1 January 1604. [Howff]
**ROBERTSON, DAVID,** a maltman in Dundee, 1612. [RPCS.IX.385]
**ROBERTSON, DAVID,** son of David Robertson, a cordiner on the Hill of Dundee, 1639. [NAS.RS35.S2.1.437]
**ROBERTSON, GEORGE,** a seaman from Dundee in Dutch service, 1636. [GAR.ONA.196.132.249]

**ROBERTSON, JAMES,** born 1555, minister of the South Kirk from 1588 to 1623. Husband of Margaret Scrymgeour, parents of Alexander and Maxwell. [F.5.319]

**ROBERTSON, JAMES,** a cordiner on the Hill of Dundee, son of William Robertson a cordiner there, 1653. [NAS.RS35.S2.IV.447]

**ROBERTSON, JOHN,** a weaver in Hilltown, 1699. [NAS.RS35.S3.X.202]

**ROBERTSON, JOHN,** the younger, a merchant in Dundee, 1697. [NAS.RD4.80.460]

**ROBERTSON, LEONARD,** master of the Margaret of Dundee, from Dundee to Darien in March 1700. [NAS.GD406]

**ROBERTSON, THOMAS,** in Abbot's Wynd, Dundee, 1600. [RGS.VI.1032]

**ROBERTSON, THOMAS,** a skinner in Dundee, 1611. [RPCS.IX.197]

**ROBERTSON, THOMAS,** a maltman in Dundee, husband of Margaret Shippard, 1650. [NAS.RS35.S2.III.502]

**ROBERTSON, WALTER,** born 1638, a mason burgess of Dundee, died 2 June 1684, husband of Helen Park. [Howff]

**ROBERTSON, WILLIAM,** a cordiner on the Hill of Dundee, husband of Elspeth Christie, 1637. [NAS.RS35.S2.I.9, etc]

**ROBERTSON, WILLIAM,** a goldsmith, was admitted as a journeyman of the Hammerman Incorporation of Dundee on 19 July 1668. [DA.GD.HF.HI]

**ROBESON, DAVID,** in Cowgait, Dundee, 1600, 1612. [RGS.VI.1060][WCB#190]

**ROBESON, ROBERT,** a litster burgess of Dundee, father of John, 1648. [NAS.RS35.S2.III.151]

**ROBSON, JANET,** wife of David Kynmonth a burgess of Dundee, heir to her father John Robson a baker in Dundee, 1622. [NAS.S/H]

**ROCHE, JOHN,** born 1572, a brabiner burgess of Dundee, died 10 February 1615, husband of Euphan Pye, 16.. (?) [Howff]

**ROCH, JOHN,** husband of Christian, daughter of Thomas Shear a brabiner on the Hill of Dundee, 1667. [NAS.RS35.S3.III.238]

**ROCH, WILLIAM,** a weaver on the Hill of Dundee, 1676. [NAS.RS35.S3.VI.129]

**RODGER, CHRISTOPHER,** in Dundee, father of John, 1664. [NAS.RS35.S3.II.136]

**RODGER, JOHN,** a merchant in Dundee, 1676. [NAS.AC7.4]
**RODGER, WALTER,** a merchant in Dundee, 1613. [DSL]
**ROGER, GEORGE,** born 1578, a mariner burgess of Dundee, died 1 October 1611, husband of Elisabeth Lochmalony, testament, 1612, Comm. Brechin. [NAS][Howff]
**ROLLAND, GILBERT,** in Abbot's Wynd, Dundee, 1600. [RGS.VI.1032]
**ROLLAND, ROBERT,** in Dundee, 1609. [RGS.VI.148]
**ROLLOCK, DAVID,** in Flukergait, Dundee, 1601; in Murraygait, Dundee, 1611; a merchant burgess of Dundee, 1612. [RGS.VI.464/1193][DSL]
**ROLLOCK, JAMES,** in Dundee, 1612. [RPCS.IX.385]
**ROLLOCK, JAMES,** of Monkisholm, and spouse Margaret Goldman, 1644. [LC#2352]
**ROLLOCK, JOHN,** master of the Pelican of Dundee, 1612, master of the William of Dundee, 1614; a merchant sailor of Dundee, husband of Elspeth Traill, 1631. [DSL][NAS.RS35.S1.VIII.226]
**ROLLOCK, RICHARD,** in Dundee, 1600. [RGS.VI.1032]
**ROLLOCK, ROBERT,** a merchant and sailor in Dundee, husband of Elspeth Traill, father of Robert, 1653. [NAS.RS35.S2.IV.101, etc]
**ROLLOCK, WALTER,** a merchant bailie of Dundee, 1610, 1620, husband of Janet Blyth. [RPCS.IX.50][NAS.RS35.S1.I.120]
**ROSS, ALEXANDER,** a merchant burgess of Dundee, 1612. [DSL]
**ROSS, ANDREW,** master of the Elspet of Dundee, 1614. [DSL]
**ROSS, ELIZABETH,** co-heir to her father Andrew Ross a mariner burgess of Dundee, 1631. [NAS.S/H]
**ROSS, GRISSEL,** co-heir to her father Andrew Ross a mariner burgess of Dundee, 1631. [NAS.S/H]
**ROSS, MARGARET,** co-heir to her father Andrew Ross a mariner burgess of Dundee, 1631. [NAS.S/H]
**ROSS, MARIOTA,** co-heir to her father Andrew Ross a mariner burgess of Dundee, 1631. [NAS.S/H]
**ROSS, THOMAS,** a merchant in Dundee and master of the Fortune of Dundee, 1678, 1687, 1688. [NAS.AC7.4; AC7.8; RD3.69.275]
**RUSSELL, GILBERT,** heir to William Moyes a bucklemaker in the Hill of Dundee, 1615. [NAS.S/H]
**SANDERS, JOHN,** a seaman from Dundee in Dutch service, testament, 30 April 1630. [GAR.ONA.190.173.263]

**SANDERSON, ALEXANDER,** from Dundee, was admitted as a burgess of Bergen, Norway, in 1615. [SAB]

**SATIRE, DAVID,** a flesher burgess of Dundee, husband of Margaret Gourlay, born 1574, died 13 December 1613. [Howff]

**SCHEWAN, DAVID,** a merchant burgess of Dundee, 1612, 1615. [DSL]

**SCOTT, JOHN,** dean of guild in Dundee, 1685. [RPCS.XI.62]

**SCOTT, JOHN, jr.** a merchant in Dundee, 1699. [NAS.RD4.84.784]

**SCOTT, PATRICK,** master of the James of Dundee, 1614. [DSL]

**SCOTT, THOMAS,** a bailie of Dundee, father of Christina, Grisel, and Martha, 1653. [NAS.RS35.S2.IV.194]

**SCRIMGEOUR, ELIZABETH,** heir to her father James Scrimgeour a burgess of Dundee, 17 March 1666. [NAS.S/H]

**SCRIMGEOUR, HENRY,** son of David Scrimgeour of Bowhill, minister of St Mary's, 1664 to 1690. Husband of Janet Alexander. [F.5.316]

**SCRIMGEOUR, Sir JAMES,** of Dudhope, constable and provost of Dundee, 1600. [RGS.VI.1060][NAS.RS35.S2.III.408]

**SCRIMGEOUR, JAMES,** a merchant burgess in Flukergait, Dundee, dead by 1601. [LC#1417]

**SCRIMGEOUR, JAMES,** bailie of Dundee, 1644. [LC#2352]

**SCRIMGEOUR, JOHN,** a merchant burgess in Flukergait, Dundee, 1601. [LC#1417]

**SCRIMGEOUR, JOHN,** born 1611, merchant and provost, died in August 1657, husband of Catherine Wright, born 1613, died 30 May 1675, parents of William, born 1641, a minister, died 14 September 1666, and John. [Howff]

**SCRIMGEOUR, JOHN,** a merchant in Dundee, 1678, 1699. [NAS.AC7.4; RD2.82.461]

**SELLAR, DAVID,** on the Hill of Dundee, father of Isabel, 1670. [NAS.RS35.S2.IV.528]

**SELLAR, JAMES,** a maltman on the Hill of Dundee, husband of Margaret Burnes, 1656. [NAS.RS35.S2.V.137]

**SHEAR, THOMAS,** a brabiner on the Hill of Dundee, father of Isobel and Margaret wife of James Mylne, and grandfather of William Mylne a weaver there, 1644. [NAS.RS35.S2.II.532; S3.III.238]

**SHEARER, JOHN,** a merchant in Dundee, father of William Shearer a merchant there, 1666. [NAS.RS35.S3.III.34]

**SHIPPARD, ANDREW,** a baxter in Dundee, husband of Margaret Rae, 1637. [NAS.RS35.S2.I.37, etc]

**SHIPPARD, ANDREW,** a chaplain at the Wellgate, 1637.
[NAS.RS35.S2.I.5]

**SIMMER, ALEXANDER,** a burgess of Dundee, son of Alexander Simmer burgess thereof, 1642. [NAS.RS35.S2.II.316]

**SIMMER, ALEXANDER,** a merchant of Dundee, husband of Elisabeth Shewan, 1642. [NAS.RS35.S2.II.316]

**SIMMER, GEORGE,** son of Alexander, a burgess of Dundee, 1642. [NAS.RS35.S2.II.316]

**SIMPSON, ANDREW,** a bonnetmaker on the Hill of Dundee, son of Patrick Simpson there, 1661. [NAS.RS35.S3.I.143]

**SIMPSON, JAMES,** a merchant of Dundee, husband of Marion Cockburn, 1642. [NAS.RS35.S2.II.60, etc]

**SIMPSON, JAMES,** son of James Simpson, a bailie of Dundee, 1698. [NAS.RS35.S3.X.82]

**SIMPSON, PATRICK,** on the Hill of Dundee, 1661. [NAS.RS35.S3.I.143, etc]

**SIMPSON, ROBERT,** a merchant in Dundee, husband of Margaret Mudie, 1642. [NAS.RS35.S2.II.60]

**SIMSON, WILLIAM,** born 1548, a merchant burgess of Dundee, husband of Barbara F...., born 1549, both died in September 1608. [Howff]

**SIMSON, WILLIAM,** a merchant in Dundee, husband of Matilda Jack, 1667. [NAS.RS35.S3.III.322]

**SKINNER, ROBERT,** in Dundee pre 1601. [RGS.VI.1187]

**SMALL, WILLIAM,** a burgess of Dundee, 1599. [RGS.VI.901]

**SMART, DAVID,** a flesher and merchant in Dundee, father of Helen, 1656. [NAS.RS35.S2.V.153, etc]

**SMART, JAMES,** master of the St Willo of Dundee, 1614. [DSL]

**SMART, JOHN,** from Dundee, a burgess of Bergen, Norway, by 1639. [SAB]

**SMART, PATRICK,** a flesher in Dundee, 1656. [NAS.RS35.S2.V.153]

**SMEATON, ANDREW,** a merchant skipper in Dundee, husband of Euphan Watson, 1697. [NAS.RD4.80.357]

**SMEATON, JAMES,** a merchant in Dundee, husband of Isabel, daughter of George Gardyn a merchant in Dundee, 1699. [NAS.RS35.S3.X.187]

**SMEATON, JOSEPH,** skipper in Dundee, husband of Marjorie Stratton, 1694. [NAS.RS35.S3.IX.259]

**SMITH, ANDREW,** born 1584, burgess and deacon of the hammerman trade of Dundee, died 24 November 1645, husband of Catharine Smythe, father of William. [Howff][NAS.RS35.S2.IV.426]

**SMITH, ARCHIBALD,** a smith on the Hill of Dundee, 1637. [NAS.RS35.S2.I.63]

**SMITH, DONALD,** was apprenticed to Thomas Lindsay, a goldsmith in Dundee, on 9 January 1668. [DA.GD.HF.HI]

**SMITH, GEORGE,** born 1667, a clockmaker in Dundee, 1688, died 10 August 1719. [NAS.RD2.69.203][Howff]

**SMITH, JAMES,** in Dundee, 1614. [DSL]

**SMITH, JOHN,** a tailor in Dundee, husband of Catherine Kynneir, 1637. [NAS.RS35.S2.I.63, etc]

**SMITH, PATRICK,** a litster in Dundee, 1688. [NAS.RD3.67.487]

**SMITH, ROBERT,** a brewster on the Hill of Dundee, husband of Elisabeth Brown, 1644. [NAS.RS35.S2.II.533]

**SMITH, THOMAS,** born 1588, deacon of the hammermen and burgess of Dundee, died 3 May 1645, husband of Marion Paterson, testament, 1645, Comm. Brechin. [NAS][Howff] [NAS.RS35.S2.IV.57]

**SMITH, WALTER,** a mealmaker in Dundee, husband of Barbara Boyes, 1637. [NAS.RS35.S2.I.49]

**SMITH, WILLIAM,** a merchant in Dundee, 1665. [NAS.RS35.S3.II.272]

**SMITH, WILLIAM,** a weaver on the Hill of Dundee, 1692. [NAS.RS35.S3..IX.51]

**SOUTAR, ROBERT,** born 1645, a mariner in Dundee, died 26 October 1709, husband of Elspet Scot. [Howff]

**SOUTAR, THOMAS,** a merchant in Dundee, 1684. [NAS.AC7/6]

**SPALDING, JOHN,** born circa 1631, minister of the Second Charge from 1691 to 1699, died before 29 March 1699. Husband of Jean Hunter, parents of Marjory, Mary, and Catherine. [F.5.320]

**SPENCE, PATRICK,** skinner in Dundee, 1611. [RPCS.IX.197]

**SPENS, EDWARD,** born 1574, a bonnet-maker burgess of Dundee, died 24 February 1644, father of Barbara and George. [Howff][NAS.RS35.S1.VIII.240]

**SPENS, GEORGE,** a bonnet-maker on the Hill of Dundee, deacon of the bonnet-makers of Dundee, husband of Agnes Barrie, parents of Isobel, 1631. [NAS.RS35.S1.VIII.240]

**SPENS, PATRICK,** a skinner in Dundee, father of Janet and Margaret, 1654. [NAS.RS35.S2.IV.450]

**STEEL, THOMAS,** born 1623, a merchant, died 14 February 1686, husband of Christian Gray, testament, 1686, Comm. Brechin. [NAS][Howff]

**STEINSON, ANDREW,** a merchant burgess in Flukergait, Dundee, 1603, husband of Margaret Green, born 1546, died 28 May 1609, testament, 1610, Comm. Brechin.[NAS][RGS.VI.1193][Howff]

**STEVENSON, ANDREW,** a skinner in Dundee, husband of Margaret Kyd, 1645. [NAS.RS35.S2.II.547]

**STEVENSON, DAVID,** a skinner in Dundee, husband of Janet Murison, father of Janet, and Margaret, 1654. [NAS.RS35.S2.IV.306]

**STEVENSON, JOHN,** a litster in Dundee, husband of Magdalene Drummond, 1631. [NAS.RS35.S1.VIII.276]

**STEVENSON, ROBERT,** a merchant in Dundee, husband of Catharine Smyth, 1653. [NAS.RS35.S2.IV.30]

**STEVENSON, WALTER,** skinner in Dundee, 1611. [RPCS.IX.197]

**STEVENSON, WILLIAM,** skinner in Dundee, 1611, husband of Grissell Thomson, born 1574, died 30 June 1632, testament, 1633, Comm. Brechin. [RPCS.IX.197][NAS][Howff]

**STEVENSON, WILLIAM,** a skinner in Dundee, husband of Janet, daughter of Andrew Morrison, 1654. [NAS.RS35.S2.IV.306]

**STEVENSON, WILLIAM,** in Dundee, dead by 1666. [RGS.XI.883]

**STEWART, JAMES,** town councillor of Dundee, 1685. [RPCS.XI.62[

**STIBBLES, ROBERT,** reader of Dundee, husband of Agnes Innes, parents of James, 1638. [NAS.RS35.S2.I.227]

**STIRLING, ISABELLA,** relict of James Kinloch a merchant in Dundee, 1688. [NAS.RD4.63.705]

**STIRLING, JOHN,** from Dundee, married Clara Maartsen in Haarlem, Holland, on 16 October 1601. [Haarlem Marriage Register]

**STIRLING, JOHN,** a merchant in Dundee, dead by 1676. [NAS.AC7.4]

**STIRLING, ROBERT,** born 1593, a merchant skipper, died 1668, husband of Euphemia Lochmalony, born 1612, died 1648, parents of John. [Howff][NAS.RS35.S3.III.445]

**STORRAR, JOHN,** a maltman in Dundee, 1676. [NAS.RS35.S3.VI.245]

**STRACHAN, DAVID,** master of the Tiger of Dundee, 1612. [DSL]

**STRACHAN, DAVID,** a goldsmith from Dundee, was admitted as a citizen of Cracow, Poland, after 1621. ['Scots in Poland', #56]

**STRACHAN, JAMES,** a notary in Argyll Street, Dundee, 1621. [LC#1891]

**STRACHAN, PATRICK,** a merchant in Dundee, 1676. [NAS.AC7.4]

**STRACHAN, ROBERT,** born 1580 a wright burgess, died 28 April 1653. [Howff]

**STRACHAN, ROBERT,** born 1620, a wright, died 15 September 1690. [Howff]

**STRAITON, ROBERT,** an apothecary in Dundee, husband of (1) Janet Duncan, born 1613, died 27 December 1652, (2) Isabel Robertson, born 1613, died 26 December 1657, father of Helen, Marjorie, and Patrick (a mariner in London), 1688. [NAS.RD4.67.480][Howff][NAS.RD35.S2.IV.198, etc]

**STURROCK, ADAM,** a mariner burgess of Dundee, husband of Elspet Elmor born 1573, died 2 August 1610, testament, 1612, Comm. Brechin. [NAS][Howff]

**STURROCK, JOHN,** born 1560, a merchant burgess of Dundee, died 1 January 1618, husband of Isobel Crockett. [Howff]

**STURROCK, JOHN,** a mariner burgess of Dundee, heir to his father John Sturrock a merchant burgess of Dundee, 1618. [NAS.S/H]

**SYME, HENRY,** a maltman in Dundee, father of Agnes, Elizabeth, and Margaret, 1631. [NAS.RS35.S1.VIII.165]

**SYME, WILLIAM,** master of the Henry of Dundee, 1680. [NAS.AC7/5]

**SYMMER, ALEXANDER,** a merchant of Dundee, 1613, husband of Margaret Fullerton, testament, 1631, Comm. Brechin. [NAS][Howff][DSL]

**SYMMER, GABRIEL,** born 1566, a cordiner, died 8 June 1614. [Howff]

**SYMSON, JAMES,** a merchant in Dundee, 1613, 1621. [DSL][WCB#185]

**TARBET, JOHN,** a merchant and bailie of Dundee, husband of Isobel Rankine, parents of Agnes, Helen, Marjorie, Robert and William, 1653. [NAS.RS35.S2.IV.70]

**THOM, JAMES,** born 1640, a merchant burgess of Dundee, died 9 November 1682, husband of Margaret Black. [Howff][NAS.RS35.S3.VI.354]

**THOM, THOMAS,** a mason in Dundee, 1685. [NAS.RS35.S3.VIII.185]

THOM, WILLIAM, a maltman in Dundee, husband of Isabel Kealman, 1637. [NAS.RS35.RS35.S2.I.31]
THOMSON, ALEXANDER, from Dundee, was admitted as a burgess of Bergen, Norway, in 1618, dead by 1635. [SAB]
THOMSON, ALEXANDER, a clothier on the Hill of Dundee, 1648. [NAS.RS35.S2.III.3]
THOMSON, DAVID, a mariner, 1597. [WCB#189]
THOMSON, GEORGE, a mealmaker on the Hill of Dundee, husband of Isobel Drummond, 1656. [NAS.RS35.S2.V.179]
THOMSON, GILBERT, son of George Thomson a mealmaker on the Hill of Dundee, 1698. [NAS.RS35.S3.X.69]
THOMSON, MATTHEW, a smith in Dundee, 1612. [RPCS.IX.385]
THOMSON, PATRICK, a wright on the Hill of Dundee, husband of Janet Sym, 1648. [NAS.RS35.S2.III.2]
THOMSON, ROBERT, in Dundee, 1614. [DSL]
THOMSON, ROBERT, a weaver in Dundee, husband of Christina, daughter of John Gibb a weaver in Pitelpie, 1667 [NAS,RS35.S3.III.242]
THORNTON, JOHN JOHNSON, from Dundee, a burgess of Bergen, Norway, in 1619. [SAB]
TINDALL, ANDREW, a maltman in Dundee, husband of Isabel Cristall, 1666. [NAS.RS35.S3.III.156]
TINDALL, DAVID, a baxter in Dundee, husband of Sarah Fullerton, 1653. [NAS.RS35.S2.IV.80]
TINDALL, DAVID, husband of Christian, daughter of Thomas Lindsay a baxter in Dundee, and son of David Tindall a baxter in Dundee, 1653. [NAS.RS35.S2.IV.80]
TINDALL, DAVID, a baxter in Dundee, husband of Margaret Stibles, son of Patrick Tindall a baxter there, 1679. [NAS.RS35.S3.VII.57, etc]
TINDALL, PATRICK, a baxter in Dundee, husband of Bessie Alison, 1656. [NAS.RS35.S2.V.227]
TODRICK, JOHN, sailor in Dundee, heir to his grandfather Thomas Fairweather a burgess of Dundee, 1634. [NAS.S/H]
TOSH, ANDREW, a merchant in Dundee, husband of Marion Ross, 1650. [NAS.RS35.S2.III.467]
TRAILL, ELIZABETH, spouse of Robert Rollock, heir portioner to her brother George Traill a merchant burgess of Dundee, 1612. [NAS.S/H]
TRAILL, JOHN, a burgess of Dundee, 1620. [NAS.RS35.S1.I.167]

**TYRIE, JOHN,** a merchant in Dundee, 1614, 1615; macer in Dundee, messenger on the Hill of Dundee, dead by 1656, husband of Magdalene Scrymgeour, 1644.
[LC#2496][DSL][NAS.RS35.S2.II.537]

**TYRIE, JOHN,** the younger, on the Hill of Dundee, son of John Tyrie and Magdalene Scrymgeour, in Dundee, 1652.
[LC#2496][NAS.RS35. S2.IV.40]

**UDWARD, ALEXANDER,** heir to his father David Udward a merchant burgess of Dundee, 1626. [NAS.S/H]

**WADDELL, JOHN,** a merchant in Dundee, 1676. [NAS.AC7.4]

**WALKER, ANDREW, a** tailor in Dundee, 1612. [RPCS.IX.385]

**WALKER, ANDREW,** a tailor in Dundee, husband of Janet Heriot, 1649. [NAS.RS35.S2.III.495]

**WALKER, JAMES,** born 1573, a merchant burgess of Dundee, died 20 March 1627, husband of Helen Simpson.
[Howff][NAS.RS35.S1.I.181]

**WALKER, JAMES,** eldest son of William Walker a skinner burgess of Dundee and Elizabeth Abercrombie, heir portioner of James Abercrombie his maternal grandfather, 1631.
[NAS.S/H][NAS.RS35.S3.I.357]

**WALKER, PETER,** a sailor in Dundee, 1643. [NAS.RS35.S2.II.164]

**WALKER, THOMAS,** in Dundee, 1601. [RGS.VI.1187]

**WALKER, THOMAS,** son of James Walker, a merchant in Dundee, 1643. [NAS.RS35.S2.II.148]

**WALKER, WILLIAM,** a skinner in Dundee, 1611. [RPCS.IX.197]

**WANDLES, DAVID,** a maltman in Dundee, 1643.
[NAS.RS35.S2.II.212]

**WANDLES, ROBERT,** a maltman in Dundee, and his son David, 1643. [NAS.RS35.S2.II.212]

**WARDROPER, ANDREW,** born 1626, a merchant in Dundee, 1676, 1688, died 23 January 1698. [NAS.AC7.4; RD4.67.187][Howff]

**WARDROPER, JOHN,** town councillor of Dundee, 1685.
[RPCS.XI.62]

**WARDROPER, THOMAS,** born 1661, a merchant and bailie of Dundee, died 21 September 1724. [Howff]

**WATSON, ALEXANDER,** a merchant in Dundee, relict Margaret Paton, 1688. [NAS.RD4.62.63]

**WATSON, ALEXANDER,** of Wallace Craigie, Provost and merchant of Dundee, husband of (1) Grisel Cochrane, (2) Margaret Lentrone, 1642. [NAS.RS35.S2.II.77, etc]

**WATSON, ANDREW,** a maltman burgess of Dundee, testament, 1678, Comm. Brechin; husband of Eupham Smart, born 1620, died 10 December 1659. [NAS][Howff]

**WATSON, BARTHOLEMEW,** in Hill of Dundee, 1649. [NAS.RS35.S2.III.394]

**WATSON, DAVID,** mason in Dundee, husband of Mary Bruce born 1650, died 29 October 1710. [Howff]

**WATSON, GILBERT,** a burgess of Dundee, heir to his father Robert Watson a mariner burgess of Dundee, 1613. [Retours]

**WATSON, JAMES,** skinner in Dundee, 1611. [RPCS.IX.197]

**WATSON, JAMES,** the younger, skinner in Dundee, 1611. [RPCS.IX.197]

**WATSON, JAMES,** a merchant burgess of Dundee, 1612, 1613. [DSL]

**WATSON, JOHN,** MD, in Dundee, son of Provost Alexander Watson of Wallace Craigie, 1673. [NAS.RS35.S3.V.222]

**WATSON, MARGARET,** daughter of Alexander Watson, son of Alexander Watson of Wallace Craigie, 1681. [NAS.RS35.S3.VII.549]

**WATSON, MARGARET,** daughter of Thomas Watson a merchant in Dundee, 1685. [NAS.RS35.S3.VIII.180]

**WATSON, MATTHEW,** born 1565, a skinner burgess of Dundee, died 9 October 1603, husband of 'I.B' born 1570, died 29 September 1608. [Howff]

**WATSON, ROBERT,** born 1605, merchant burgess, died 10 October 1641. [Howff]

**WATSON, ROBERT,** a weaver on the Hill of Dundee, husband of Jean Mealmaker, 1688. [NAS.RD4.62.766; RS35.S2.III.394, etc]

**WATSON, THOMAS,** a merchant burgess of Dundee, spouse of Elspet Alexander born 1621, died in June 1645. [Howff]

**WATSON, THOMAS,** a bailie of Dundee, 1685. [RPCS.XI.62]

**WATSON, WALTER,** a maltman in Dundee, 1653. [NAS.RS35.S2.IV.89]

**WATSON, WILLIAM,** son of Alexander Watson of Wallace Craigie, 1680. [NAS.RS35.S3.VI.419]

**WATSON, WILLIAM,** a merchant in Dundee, 1676, 1688. [NAS.AC7.4; RD3.68.291]

**WATT, ALEXANDER,** a braboner on the Hill of Dundee, husband of Catharine Smith, 1657. [NAS.RS35.S2.V.390]

**WATT, ALEXANDER,** a weaver on the Hill of Dundee, husband of Janet Fleming, 1661. [NAS.RS35.S3.I.175, etc]

**WATT, ALEXANDER,** a maltman on the Hill of Dundee, husband of (1) Isobel Liddell, (2) Mary Parrott, 1685. [NAS.RS35.S3.VIII.133, etc]

**WATT, ALEXANDER,** bailie of the barony of the Hiltown of Dundee, 1692. [NAS.RS35.S3.IX.60/567]

**WATT, ANDREW,** born 1615, a skinner burgess, died 12 April 1649. [Howff]

**WATT, DAVID,** born 1580, a skinner burgess in Dundee, 1611, died 9 February 1646. [RPCS.IX.197][Howff]

**WATT, GEORGE,** a sailor in Dundee, husband of Janet Lude, 1639. [NAS.RS35.S2.I.510]

**WATT, JAMES,** born 1579, a flesher burgess, died 26 September 1641, husband of Agnes Theane. [Howff]

**WATT, JAMES,** a weaver on the Hill of Dundee, husband of (1) Margaret Bathie, (2) Helen Smith, 1639. [NAS.RS35.S2.I.439, etc]

**WATT, JOHN,** weaver on the Hill of Dundee, husband of Janet Watt, 1698. [NAS.RS35.S3.IX.567]

**WATT, ROBERT,** a flesher in Dundee, 1662. [NAS.RS35.S2.I.511]

**WATT, WILLIAM,** a maltman on the Hill of Dundee, 1657. [NAS.RS35.S2.V.390, etc]

**WATT, WILLIAM,** shoremaster of Dundee, 1685. [RPCS.XI.62]

**WEBSTER, JAMES,** born 1669, a merchant in Dundee, died 28 March 1709, husband of Helen Wood. [Howff]

**WEBSTER, JOHN,** born 1619, a maltman burgess of Dundee, died 14 September 1663. [Howff]

**WEDDERBURN, Mr ALEXANDER,** 1618; a bailie of Dundee in 1621; heir to his father Mr James Wedderburn clerk of Dundee, 1628, 1631. [LC#1891][NAS.S/H][RGS.VI.1956;VIII.117/799][NAS.RS35.S2.VIII..247]

**WEDDERBURN, ALEXANDER,** of Easter Powrie, born 1615, late provost of Dundee, died 9 April 1683, husband of (1) Elisabeth Ramsay, born 1621, daughter of John Ramsay, died 2 April 1643, (2) Margaret Milne. [Howff][NAS.RS35.S2.I.157, etc]

**WEDDERBURN, DAVID,** a burgess of Dundee, 1600, 1612. [RGS.VI.1060][DSL]

**WEDDERBURN, DAVID,** a burgess of Dundee, 1642. [NAS.RS35.S2.II.60]

**WEDDERBURN, JAMES,** son of Alexander Wedderburn town clerk of Dundee, 1620. [RGS.VIII.799]
**WEDDERBURN, JAMES,** died 1620, husband of Mary Goldman. [Howff]
**WEDDERBURN, JAMES,** town clerk and keeper of the records of Dundee, 1685. [RPCS.XI.62]; husband of Bessie Davidson, 1638. [NAS.RS35.S3.V.198]
**WEDDERBURN, JOHN,** 1609, 1612. [RGS.VI.148][WCB#191]
**WEDDERBURN, JOHN,** son of James Wedderburn, a burgess of Dundee, 1638. [NAS.RS35.S2.I.134]
**WEDDERBURN, PATRICK,** a merchant in Dundee, husband of Elizabeth Low, 1680. [NAS.RS3.VII.341]
**WEDDERBURN, PATRICK,** a burgess of Dundee, 1638. [NAS.RS35.S2.I.157]
**WEDDERBURN, PETER,** the younger, 1612. [WCB#187]
**WEDDERBURN, PETER,** son of Alexander Wedderburn of Easter Powrie, provost of Dundee. 1676. [NAS.RS35.S3.VI.385]
**WEDDERBURN, ROBERT,** a notary in Dundee, 1609. [WCB#187]
**WEDDERBURN, ROBERT,** a merchant in Dundee, 1670. [NAS.RS35.S3.IV.505]
**WELLWOOD, JOHN,** a burgess of Dundee, supercargo (?) of the Grace of God of Dundee trading between Newfoundland and Lisbon in 1604. [SHS.4/2/X.78-80]
**WEMYSS, DAVID,** a merchant in Dundee, 1613. [DSL]
**WEMYSS, EUPHAME,** daughter of David Wemyss a merchant in Dundee, 1649. [NAS.RS35.S2.III.365]
**WEMYSS, WILLIAM,** son of William Wemyss, a bailie of Dundee, 1656. [NAS.RS35.S2.V.91]
**WEST, JOHN,** born 1630, a builder burgess, died 2 January 1707, husband of Jean Kerr, born 1658, died 8 January 1708. [Howff]
**WHITTET, WILLIAM,** a merchant in Dundee, 1686. [NAS.AC7/7]
**WHITTON, JAMES,** a maltman in Dundee, husband of Margaret Whitton, 1692. [NAS.RS35.S3.IX.302]
**WHYTE, DAVID,** a bonnet-maker on the Hill of Dundee, husband of Janet Kyd, 1654. [NAS.RS35.S2.IV.414]
**WHYTE, DAVID,** a brabiner on the Hill of Dundee, husband of Mause Robertson, 1654. [NAS.RS35.S2.IV.498, etc]
**WHYTE, JAMES,** a cordiner on the Hill of Dundee, 1653. [NAS.RS35.S2.IV.414]

**WHYTE, JAMES,** deacon convenor of the trades of Dundee, 1699. [NAS.RS35.S3.X.202]

**WHYTE, JAMES,** a weaver in Hilltown, husband of Mause Robertson, 1660. [NAS.RS35.S3.I.5]

**WHYTE, JAMES,** a sailor in Dundee, 1692. [NAS.RS35.IX.100]

**WHYTE, JOHN,** a skipper in Dundee, relict Marjorie Forrester, 1661. [NAS.RD4/4/2]

**WHYTE, JOHN,** brother of Thomas Whyte, weaver on the Hill of Dundee, 1692. [NAS.RS35.S3.IX.101]

**WHYTE, ROBERT,** a merchant in Dundee, 1698. [NAS.RS35.S3.X.47]

**WHYTE, THOMAS,** servant of Andrew Anderson, a weaver on the Hill of Dundee, 1661. [NAS.RS35.S3.I.174]

**WHYTE, WILLIAM,** a wright in Dundee, 1666. [NAS.RS35.S3.III.118]

**WHYTE, WILLIAM,** son of James Wright, a weaver on the Hill of Dundee, 1666. [NAS.RS35.S3.III.118]

**WICHTAN, GEORGE,** notary burgess of Dundee, testament, 1650, Comm. Brechin. [NAS]

**WICHTAN, THOMAS,** a notary in Dundee, and his son Alexander, 1612, 1621, 1656. husband of (1) Janet C, born 1583, died 22 August 1645, (2) Janet Mudie. [NAS.RS35.S2.IV.333] [WCB#187][RGS.VIII.1989][LC#2496][Howff]

**WILKIE, DAVID,** a weaver in Hilltown, husband of Jean Saunders, 1696. [NAS.RS35.S3.IX.522]

**WILKIE, WILLIAM,** a weaver on the Hill of Dundee, husband of Catherine Wichtan, 1692. [NAS.RS35.S3.IX.64]

**WILL, PATRICK,** a maltman in Dundee, father of Patrick who died 29 November 1703, and James who died 7 August 1709. [Howff]

**WILLIAMSON, ALEXANDER,** maltman burgess of Dundee, husband of (1) Margaret Crystall born 1640, died 28 February 1660, (2) Jean Boyack, born 1632, died 16 May 1684. [Howff]

**WILLIAMSON, DAVID,** a tailor in Hill of Dundee, 1655. [NAS.RS35.S2.V.1]

**WILLIAMSON, PATRICK,** a maltman in Dundee, 1692. [NAS.RS35.S3.IX.9]

**WILLIAMSON, PATRICK,** a merchant in Dundee, 1698. [NAS.RS35.S3.X.35]

**WILLISON, ROGER,** born 1620, weaver in Hill of Dundee, died 18 October 1681.[Howff]

**WILSON, JAMES,** a merchant in Dundee, husband of Margaret Rollock, 1649. [NAS.RS35.S2.III.152]

**WINTON, ANDREW,** feuar of Strathmartine, a burgess of Dundee, 1621. [LC#1891]

**WOOD, BARBARA,** and her spouse Robert Gray, a notary burgess of Dundee, testament, 21 February 1642, Comm. Brechin. [NAS]

**WOOD, DAVID,** a skinner burgess of Dundee, his spouse Janet Mann, and her daughter Margaret Greif, testament, 2 July 1612, Comm. Brechin. [NAS]

**WRIGHT, CATHERINE,** mother of John Scrymgeour a merchant in Dundee, 1674. [NAS.RS35.S3.V.373]

**WRIGHT, CHRISTIAN,** spouse to Gilbert Guthrie a merchant burgess of Dundee, testament, 17 October 1662, Comm. Brechin. [NAS]

**WRIGHT, CHRISTIAN,** relict of John Smith sometime a merchant burgess of Dundee, testament, 23 March 1674, Comm. Brechin. [NAS]

**WRIGHT, DAVID,** a merchant in Dundee, 1638. [NAS.RS35.S2.I.397]

**WRIGHT, GRISSELL,** 1676, [NAS.RS35.S3.VI.133]; relict of John Hunter a maltman in Dundee, testament, 1 February 1690, Comm. Brechin. [NAS]

**WRIGHT, JAMES,** a merchant in Dundee, 1661. [NAS.RD2/3/421]

**WRIGHT, Mr JAMES,** student of theology, burgess of Dundee, testament, 21 March 1667, Comm. Brechin. [NAS]

**WRIGHT, Mr JAMES,** in Dundee, testament, 23 October 1699, Comm. Brechin. [NAS]

**WRIGHT, JANET,** spouse of Thomas Constable a flesher in Dundee, 1670. [NAS.RS35.S3.IV.461]

**WRIGHT, PATRICK,** a maltman in Dundee, husband of Margaret Paul, 1676. [NAS.RS35.S3.VI.262]

**WRIGHT, PETER,** a maltman in Dundee, and his spouse Agnes Rollo, testament, 27 September 1682, Comm. Brechin. [NAS]

**WRIGHT, ROBERT,** a merchant in Dundee, 1688. [NAS.RD2.69.201]

**WRIGHT, WILLIAM,** a merchant in Dundee, 1643. [NAS.RS35.S2.II.206]

**WRIGHT, WILLIAM,** the younger, 1638, a merchant burgess of Dundee, and his spouse Euphemia Peirson, testament, 3 August 1646, Comm. Brechin. [NAS][NAS.RS35.S2.I.290, etc]

**YEAMAN, ALEXANDER,** MD in Dundee, and Margaret Ramsay his spouse, testament, 7 February 1671, Comm. Brechin. [NAS]

**YEAMAN, ALEXANDER,** doctor of medicine in Dundee, 1668, [NAS.RS35.S3.IV.13], father of Alexander and Marjorie, 1688. [NAS.RD3.68.673]

**YEAMAN, ALEXANDER,** son of Alexander Yeaman, doctor of medicine, 1676. [NAS.RS35.S3.VI.202]

**YEAMAN, CATHERINE,** spouse to Andrew Duncan a maltman burgess of Dundee, testament, 15 April 1664, Comm. Brechin. [NAS]

**YEAMAN, DAVID,** a merchant burgess of Dundee, testament, 21 February 1611, Comm. Brechin. [NAS]

**YEAMAN, DAVID,** the younger, a merchant burgess of Dundee, testaments, 25 April 1611 and 2 November 1613, Comm. Brechin. [NAS]

**YEAMAN, DAVID,** a merchant burgess of Dundee, and his spouse Marjorie Kinnaird, testaments, 16 December 1624 and 3 December 1625, Comm. Brechin. [NAS]

**YEAMAN, DAVID,** a merchant in Dundee, husband of Elizabeth Yeaman, 1649. [NAS.RS35.S2.III.315]

**YEAMAN, DAVID,** a maltman burgess of Dundee, and his relict Margaret Powrie, testament, 13 May 1657, Comm. Brechin. [NAS]

**YEAMAN, DAVID,** an apothecary in Dundee, husband of Barbara Lovell, 1666. [NAS.RS35.S3.III.156]

**YEAMAN, DAVID,** a surgeon burgess of Dundee, and his spouse Isobel Stirling, testament, 25 February 1684, Comm. Brechin. [NAS]

**YEAMAN, ISOBEL,** spouse of William Raitt, son of William Raitt, minister at Dundee, 1673. [NAS.RS35.S3.V.286]

**YEAMAN, KATHERINE,** daughter of Patrick Yeaman of Dryburgh, and spouse of Alexander Blair, dean of guild of Dundee, 1684. [NAS.RS35.S3.VIII.26]

**YEAMAN, JAMES,** a merchant burgess of Dundee, testament, 14 August 1656, Comm. Brechin. [NAS]

**YEAMAN, JAMES,** of East Mylne of Rattray, husband of Jean Cargill, born 1634, died 1 January 1706. [Howff]

**YEAMAN, JANET,** daughter of the late William Yeaman a merchant burgess of Dundee, testament, 30 April 1632, Comm. Brechin. [NAS]

**YEAMAN, JOHN,** of Dryburgh, 1628. [Howff]
**YEAMAN, JOHN,** of Dryburgh, a merchant in Dundee, 1631. [NAS.RS35.S1.VIII.236]
**YEAMAN, JOHN,** son of the late William Yeaman a merchant burgess of Dundee, testament, 30 April 1632, Comm. Brechin. [NAS]
**YEAMAN, MARGARET,** daughter of John Yeaman, a merchant in Dundee, and his spouse Margaret Yeaman, testament, 26 January 1627, Comm. Brechin. [NAS]
**YEAMAN, MARGARET,** relict of George Fernie late bailie of Dundee, testament, 22 February 1684, Comm. Brechin. [NAS]
**YEAMAN, MARION,** daughter of Patrick Yeaman of Dryburgh, and spouse of Robert Watson a merchant in Dundee, 1684. [NAS.RS35.S3.VIII.27]
**YEAMAN, PATRICK,** the elder, a merchant burgess of Dundee, husband of Christian Rodger who died 10 July 1603. [Howff]
**YEAMAN, PATRICK,** of Dryburgh, a burgess of Dundee, and his spouse, testament, 22 July 1626, Comm. Brechin. [NAS]
**YEAMAN, PATRICK,** a merchant in Dundee, 1644. [NAS.RS35.S2.II.552]
**YEAMAN, Mr PATRICK,** in Dundee, testaments, 11 January and 6 October 1677, Comm. Brechin. [NAS]
**YEAMAN, PATRICK,** bailie of Dundee, husband of Margaret Paterson, testaments, 28 November 1704 & 5 June 1707, Comm. Brechin. [NAS]
**YEAMAN, ROBERT,** son of the late David Yeaman, a merchant burgess of Dundee, testament, 30 April 1632, Comm. Brechin. [NAS]
**YEAMAN, WILLIAM,** a merchant burgess of Dundee, and his spouse Alison Liddell, testament, 16 October 1624, Comm. Brechin. [NAS]
**YOUNG, JAMES,** son of James Young a maltman in Dundee, 1620. [NAS.RS35.S1.I.120]
**YOUNG, JANET,** daughter of Alexander Young a bonnetmaker, granddaughter of James Richardson a bonnetmaker on the Hill of Dundee, and spouse of Thomas Millar a bonnetmaker there, 1661. [NAS.RS35.S3.I.35]
**YOUNG, JEAN,** daughter of Alexander Young a bonnetmaker, granddaughter of James Richardson a bonnetmaker on the Hill of

Dundee, and spouse of George Mitchell a bonnetmaker there, 1661. [NAS.RS35.S3.I.35]

**YOUNG, JOHN,** a merchant in Dundee, husband of Elizabeth Clerk, father of Thomas, 1631. [NAS.RS35.S1.VIII.269]

**YOUNG, MARJORIE,** relict of John Peebles, son of Robert Peebles in Westfield of Dundee, and spouse of John Schewan, 1653. [NAS.RS35.S2.IV.418]

**YOUNG, THOMAS,** in Dundee, 1601; born 1566, a merchant, died 2 March 1610, husband of Margaret Fyfe, testament, 10 May 1610, Comm. Brechin. [RGS.VI.1187][Howff][NAS]

# INTRODUCTION

This publication is designed as an aid to local historians and genealogists wishing to find information on the inhabitants of Dundee during the eighteenth century. It is based overwhelmingly on primary sources, such as the records of the High Court of the Admiralty of Scotland, the Commissary Court of Brechin, the Customs and Excise, the Exchequer, the Register of Deeds of the Court of Session, the Royal Burgh of Dundee, the Services of Heirs, the Register of Sasines of Forfarshire, and Howff monumental inscriptions, located in the National Archives of Scotland in Edinburgh and Dundee Archive and Record Centre.

This does not claim to be an exhaustive list of the inhabitants of Dundee but rather an illustration of some of the records available. Each entry is fully referenced and should provide material of interest to the family historian.

David Dobson

St Andrews, 2008

## REFERENCES

| | | |
|---|---|---|
| CB | = | Commissariat of Brechin, Register of Testaments |
| DCA | = | Dundee Archive and Record Centre |
| | B | = Burgh Records |
| HMI | = | Howff Monumental Inscription |
| JA | = | Jacobites of Angus, 1689-1746 |
| NA | = | National Archives |
| | AO | = Audit Office |
| | T | = Treasury |
| NAS | = | National Archives of Scotland |
| | AC | = Admiralty Court |
| | CC | = Commissary Court |
| | CH | = Church |
| | CS | = Court of Session |
| | E | = Exchequer |
| | RD | = Register of Deeds |
| | RS | = Register of Sasines |
| | SC | = Sheriff Court |
| NEHGS | | New England Historic Genealogical Society |
| NRAS= | | National Register of Archives, Scotland |

# THE PEOPLE OF DUNDEE,

## 1700-1799

**ABBOT, JANET,** b. 1752, wife of William Wilkie in Lochee, d. 1814. [HMI]
**ABBOT, WILLIAM,** flesher in the Hill of Dundee, testament, 1763, C.B. [NAS]
**ABBOT, WILLIAM,** carter in Dundee, wife Grizel Elder, sasine,1769. [NAS.RS35.22.489]
**ABERCROMBIE, DAVID,** merchant in Dundee, son of James Abercrombie a skipper there, sasine, 1734. [NAS.RS35.15.127]
**ABERCROMBIE, JAMES,** skipper in Dundee, a bond, 1739. [NRAS.150.3.20]
**ABERCROMBIE, THOMAS,** master of the George of Dundee, 1711; bailie of Dundee, 1715; boxmaster of the Fraternity of Seamen in Dundee, 1725. [NAS.RD3.144.445; AC9.378/945]
**ABERCROMBIE, WILLIAM,** skipper of Dundee, boxmaster of the Fraternity of Seamen there, 1704. [NAS.AC8.23]
**ADAM, DAVID,** b.1751, skipper in Dundee, d.1797. [HMI]
**ADAM, JOHN,** mate of the Samuel of Dundee, 1744. [NAS.AC11.159]
**AFFLECK, GILBERT,** litster in Dundee, 1701. [NAS.RD2.85.396]
**AFFLECK, JAMES,** merchant in Dundee, 1715. [NAS.RD2.104.544; RD3.145.480; RD4.117.915]
**AFFLECK, JOHN,** merchant in Dundee, 1701. [NAS.RD4.89.419]
**ALEXANDER, JAMES,** formerly a preacher & schoolmaster in Eassie, then in Dundee, testament, 1796, C.B. [NAS]
**ALISON, JAMES,** merchant of Dundee, 1713. [NAS.AC8.159]
**ALISON, JANET,** relict of Thomas Bower a merchant & Provost of Dundee, testament, 1742, C.B. [NAS]
**ALISON, WILLIAM,** merchant in Dundee, 1715. [NAS.RD4.117.379]
**ALISON, WILLIAM,** merchant & bailie of Dundee, 1748, testament, 1758, 1762, C.B. [NAS.E326.1.50]
**ALLAN, JOHN,** skipper in Dundee, 1717. [NAS.AC13.1.91]
**ALLAN, JOHN,** in Dundee, testament, 1747, C.B. [NAS]

# THE PEOPLE OF DUNDEE, 1700-1799

**ALLAN, JOHN,** b. 1735, wigmaker in Dundee, d. 1804. [HMI]
**ALLAN, ROBERT,** coppersmith in Dundee, testament, 1743, C.B. [NAS]
**ALLAN, WILLIAM,** skipper in Dundee, testament, 1738, C.B.
**ANDERSON, ALEXANDER,** merchant in Dundee, 1748, testament, 1756, C.B. [NAS.E326.1.50]
**ANDERSON, ANDREW,** mariner in Dundee, late mate of the Gloucester of Dundee, 1734. [NAS.AC8.500]
**ANDERSON, DAVID,** merchant & later a cotton manufacturer in Dundee, 1793. [DCA.B19.3.27/228]
**ANDERSON, DAVID,** merchant & shoemaker in Dundee, testament, 1793, C.B. [NAS]
**ANDERSON, JAMES,** weaver in Dundee, 1748. [NAS.E326.1.50]
**ANDERSON, ROBERT,** seaman on the James of Dundee, 1716. [NAS.AC9.565]
**ANDERSON, ROBERT,** skipper of the Margaret of Dundee, 1746. [NAS.AC8.664]
**ANDERSON, THOMAS,** b.1720, brewer in Dundee, testament, 1748. [NAS.E326.1.50][HMI]
**ANDERSON, WILLIAM,** mealmaker in Dundee, 1772. [NAS.CH2.2118.67]
**ANGUS, CHARLES,** carpenter in Dundee, 1734; shipbuilder in Dundee, testament, 1743, 1744, C.B. [NAS.AC8.494/514]
**ANGUS, JAMES,** a maltman in Dundee, testament, 1756, C.B.
**ARBUTHNOTT, CHRISTIAN,** relict of Lieutenant William Fenton, sometime resident if Dundee, testament, 1752, C.B.
**ARCHER, PETER,** at Greenfauld, by West Port of Dundee, testament, 1780, C.B. [NAS]
**ARROT, MARGARET,** relict of John Willieson late minister in Dundee, testament, 1758, C.B. [NAS]
**ARROTT, THOMAS,** in Dundee, 1748. [NAS.E326.1.50]
**AUCHENLECK, DAVID,** vintner in Dundee, 1745; in Dundee, 1748. [NAS.E326.1.50] [JA]
**AUCHENLECK, DAVID,** merchant in Dundee, testament, 1775, C.B. [NAS]
**AUCHENLECK, JAMES,** merchant in Dundee, 1716; testament, 1717, C.B. [NAS.AC9.566]
**AUCHENLECK, Mrs,** in Dundee, 1748. [NAS.E326.1.50]

# THE PEOPLE OF DUNDEE, 1700-1799

**AUCHTERLONIE, ALEXANDER,** merchant in Dundee, 1701. [NAS.RDD2.85.394]
**AUCHTERLONIE, Madam,** in Dundee, 1748. [NAS.E326.1.50]
**BAILLIE, GEORGE,** bonnetmaker in Dundee, 1745. [JA]
**BAILLIE, THOMAS,** master of the Joseph of Dundee, 1728. [NAS.AC10.132]
**BAILLIE, THOMAS,** wright in Dundee, testament, 1784, C.B.. [NAS]
**BAIN, WALTER,** mason in Wellgate, Dundee, 1796. [DCA.B19.3.26/1]
**BALLINGALL, ALEXANDER,** surgeon apothecary in Dundee, 1701. [NAS.RD4.89.6]
**BALLINGALL, DAVID,** writer in Dundee, 1757. [NRAS.150.3.25]
**BALLINGALL, JAMES,** b. 1730, minister in Dundee, d. 1763.
**BALLINGALL, JOHN,** merchant in Dundee, 1715. [NAS.RD3.144.49; RD4.117.463]
**BALLINGALL, JOHN,** bailie of Dundee, 1748. [NAS.E356.1.50]
**BALLINGAL, OLIVER,** mariner in Dundee, 1714. [NAS.AC11.12]
**BALNAVES, PATRICK,** merchant & bailie of Dundee, 1703, 1715, testament 1735, 1738, C.B. [NAS.AC6.1; RD4.116.398]
**BALVAIRD, DAVID,** bailie of Dundee, 1715. [NAS.RD4.116.568]
**BALVAIRD, ROBERT,** merchant in Dundee, 1701, 1715. [NAS.RD4.89.447; RD4.116.175]
**BALVAIRD, Mrs,** in Dundee, 1748. [NAS.E326.1.50]
**BARCLAY, JOHN,** skipper bailie of Dundee, 1744; 1748; late provost & shipmaster, testament, 1766, C.B.. [NAS.E326.1.50; CS16.1.75]
**BARCLAY, JOHN,** brewer in Dundee, 1748. [NAS.E326.1.50]
**BARCLAY, OLIVER,** merchant in Dundee, 1715. [NAS.RD2.105.187]
**BARCLAY, THOMAS,** weaver in Dundee, 1748. [NAS.E326.1.50]
**BARON, THOMAS,** baker in Dundee, d.1755, wife Margaret Knight. [HMI]
**BARRIE, JOHN,** skipper in Dundee, testament, 1775, C.B.

# THE PEOPLE OF DUNDEE, 1700-1799

**BARRON, HELEN,** spouse of Andrew Mores wheelwright in the Hill of Dundee, testament, 1751, C.B. [NAS]

**BATCHELOR, WILLIAM,** weaver in Hawkhill, wife Margaret Mudie, b.1779, d.1806. [HMI]

**BATHGATE, EUPHEMIA,** relict of Robert Lauder the clerk-depute of Dundee, testament, 1718, C.B. [NAS]

**BAXTER, ALEXANDER,** b. 1723, d. 1796, wife Margaret Mitchell, b. 1734, d. 1801. [HMI]

**BAXTER, ANDREW,** master of the Carstairs of Dundee, 1733. [NAS.AC8.473]

**BEATON, JOHN,** Customs collector at Dundee, 1701. [NAS.RD2.85.266]

**BEG, ANDREW,** wright in Dundee, testament, 1749, C.B. [NAS]

**BEG, ROBERT,** merchant in Dundee, testament, 1774, C.B. [NAS]

**BEIG, ALEXANDER,** b. 1737, manufacturer in Hilltown, d.1819, wife Catherine Thom, b.1752, d.1811. [HMI]

**BEIG, JANET,** b.1740, d.1785. [HMI]

**BELL, ALEXANDER,** late bailie of Dundee, disposition, 1714. [NRAS.2148/8/11]

**BELL, ALEXANDER,** b. 1770, shipmaster in Dundee, d. 1808. [HMI]

**BELL, DAVID,** tide surveyor at Dundee, 1723. [NAS.AC9.813]

**BELL, JOHN,** wright in Dundee, testament, 1763, C.B. [NAS]

**BELL, SAMUEL,** b.1740, architect in Dundee, d.1813. [HMI]

**BELL, WILLIAM,** skipper in Dundee, testament, 1708, C.B.; his widow Barbara Taylor, 1712. [NAS.AC9.427]

**BELL, WILLIAM,** b. 1720, shipmaster in Dundee, d. 1774. [HMI]

**BENNET, ALEXANDER,** b.1689, mason, d.1753, wife Isobel Scott, b.1695, d.1770. [HMI]

**BERRIE, ANDREW,** shipmaster in Dundee, testament, 1756, C.B. [NAS]

**BERRY, JAMES,** builder in Dundee, wife Amelia watt, b.1745, d.1804. [HMI]

**BEVERIDGE, ALEXANDER,** writer in Dundee, testament, 1770, C.B. [NAS]

**BEVERIDGE, ANNA,** relict of .... Fauld maltman in Dundee, testament, 1755, C.B. [NAS]

# THE PEOPLE OF DUNDEE, 1700-1799

**BINNIE, JANET,** relict of David Simpson weaver in Dundee, testament, 1777, C.B. [NAS]
**BINNIE, WILLIAM,** ale-seller in Dundee, testament, 1782, C.B.
**BIRRELL, JAMES,** former master of the Margaret of Dundee, 1746. [NAS.AC8.670]
**BIRRELL, MARGARET,** daughter of the late Robert Birrell a shipmaster in Dundee, testament, 1795, C.B.. [NAS]
**BIRRELL, ROBERT,** born 1693, skipper in Dundee, d.1726. [HMI]
**BIRRELL, THOMAS,** merchant in Dundee, 1745. [JA]
**BIRRELL, Mrs,** in Dundee, 1748. [NAS.E326.1.50]
**BISSET, WILLIAM,** merchant in Dundee, 1798. [DCA.B19.3.27/8]
**BLACK, ANDREW,** b.1722, d.1780, wife Ann Galloway. b.1722, d.1777. [HMI]
**BLACK, JOHN,** shipmaster in Dundee, testament, 1737, C.B.
**BLACK, KATHERINE,** spouse of John Glass a minister in Dundee, testament, 1752, C.B. [NAS]
**BLACK, MARGARET,** relict of Patrick Smyth litster in Dundee, testament, 1706, C.B. [NAS]
**BLACK, THOMAS,** surgeon in Dundee, 1748. [NAS.E326.1.50]
**BLAIR, ALEXANDER,** merchant & provost of Dundee, 1701, 1706, testament, 1717, C.B.[NAS.RD3.95.442; AC9.195]
**BLAIR, Reverend GEORGE,** in Dundee, 1748. [NAS.E326.1.50]
**BLAIR, JAMES,** corkcutter in Dundee, testament, 1750, C.B.
**BLAIR, JAMES,** b.1691, maltman in Dundee, d.1755, wife Mary McLaren, b.1680, d.1754. [HMI]
**BLAIR, JOHN,** apothecary in Dundee, 1701. [NAS.RD4.89.722]
**BLAIR, JOHN,** of Balmytie, merchant burgess of Dundee, testament, 1709, C.B.[NAS]
**BLAIR, JOHN,** MD in Dundee, 1715; testament, 1733, 1738, C.B. [NAS.RS4.117.379]
**BLAIR, JOHN,** brewer in Chapelshade, Dundee, testament, 1777, C.B. [NAS]
**BLAIR, THOMAS,** merchant from Dundee, probate 1767 New York
**BLAIR, WILLIAM,** brewer in Dundee, 1748. [NAS.E326.1.50]
**BLENSHALL, JAMES,** mariner in Dundee, 1774. [NAS.CS16.1.157/399]

# THE PEOPLE OF DUNDEE, 1700-1799

**BLYTH, CHARLES,** mariner in Dundee, testament, 1775, C.B.
**BLYTH, JOHN,** merchant in Dundee, 1748. [NAS.E326.1.50]
**BLYTHE, JOHN,** skipper in Dundee, 1750; testament, 1764, C.B. [NAS.AC11.189]
**BLYTH, ROBERT,** skipper in North Ferry, testament, 1702, C.B. [NAS]
**BLYTHE, THOMAS,** merchant in Dundee, 1706. [NAS.AC9.216]
**BLYTHE, THOMAS,** skipper of Dundee, 1711, master of the Elizabeth of North Ferry, 1711. [NAS.AC8.126; AC9.393]
**BLYTH, WILLIAM,** in Dundee, testament, 1709, C.B. [NAS]
**BORTHWICK, ALEXANDER,** writer in Dundee, 1796. [DCA.B19.3.26/5]
**BOWER, ALEXANDER,** skipper of the Alexander of Dundee captured by a French privateer, 1706, 1715. [NAS.AC9.209; AC9.540]
**BOWER, ALEXANDER,** merchant & late Dean of Guild of Dundee, testament, 1721, C.B.. [NAS]
**BOWER, THOMAS,** merchant in Dundee, 1701, 1704. [NAS.RD4.89.353; AC9.65]
**BOWMAN, ALEX&ER,** waulker in Dundee, testament, 1741, C.B.. [NAS]
**BOWMAN, DAVID,** weaver in Dundee, testament, 1772, C.B.. [NAS]
**BOWMAN, GEORGE,** shipmaster in Dundee, & spouse Alison Pattullo, 1799. [DCA.B19.3.27/172]
**BOYACK, MARGARET,** relict of George Spankie late barber & wigmaker in Dundee, daughter of the late John Boyack merchant in Dundee, testament, 1772, C.B. [NAS]
**BOYACK, THOMAS,** maltman in Dundee, wife Janet Smith, d.1715. [HMI]
**BOYAR, JAMES,** maltman in Dundee, 1706. [NAS.AC8.65]
**BOYTER, DAVID,** shipmaster in Dundee, testament, 1792, C.B.
**BR&, ROBERT,** gardener in Dundee, testament, 1759, C.B.
**BRISBANE, DAVID,** of Bullion, writer in Dundee, 1725, 1734, 1748. [NAS.AC9.943; AC8.500; E326.1.50]
**BROWN, ALEXANDER,** maltman in Dundee, 1701. [NAS.RD4.88.638]
**BROWN, ALEXANDER,** brewer in Dundee, 1748. [NAS.E326.1.50]

# THE PEOPLE OF DUNDEE, 1700-1799

**BROWN, ANDREW,** wright in Dundee, 1748. [NAS.E326.1.50]
**BROWN, DAVID,** merchant in Dundee, 1706, 1708, 1714, testament, C.B. [NAS.AC9.238; AC8.100]
**BROWN, GEORGE,** son of the late David Brown merchant in Dundee, testament, 1721, C.B. [NAS]
**BROWN, JAMES,** tailor in Dundee, 1745. [JA]
**BROWN, JAMES,** skipper in Dundee, 1748. [NAS.E326.1.50]
**BROWN, JOHN,** maltman in Dundee, spouse Margaret Thom, 1707. [NAS.AC9.247]
**BROWN, JOHN,** skipper in Dundee, 1715, 1725. [NAS.RD3.144.318; AC9.891]
**BROWN, Dr JOHN,** in Dundee, 1748. [NAS.E326.1.50]
**BROWN, JOHN,** of Glasswell, merchant in Dundee, testament, 1748, C.B. [NAS.E326.1.50]
**BROWN, JOHN, jr.,** merchant in Dundee, 1745. [JA]
**BROWN, JOHN,** in Pleasants, Dundee, testament, 1769, C.B.
**BROWN, JOHN,** merchant in Dundee, testament, 1794, C.B.
**BROWN, JOHN,** ship carpenter in Dundee, testament, 1796, C.B. [NAS]
**BROWN, MARGARET,** in Dundee, relict of James McRobie, testament, 1799, C.B. [NAS]
**BROWN, MATTHEW,** merchant trading between Dundee & Carolina, 1773. [NAS.E504.11.8]
**BROWN, PATRICK,** feuar in Blackscroft, testament, 1793, C.B. [NAS]
**BROWN, PATRICK,** apprentice to the Town Clerk of Dundee, 1796. [DCA.B19.3.26/7]
**BROWN, THOMAS,** shipmaster in Dundee, testament, 1792, C.B. [NAS]
**BROWN, WILLIAM,** bellman in Dundee, 1706. [NAS.AC9.216]
**BRUCE, ALEXANDER,** vintner in Dundee, 1701. [NAS.RD2.85.218]
**BRUCE, DAVID,** wife Grissell Watson, merchant in Dundee, 1715; testament, 1723, C.B. [NAS.RD2.104.625][HMI]
**BRUCE, GEORGE,** rector of Dundee Grammar School, testament, 1740, C.B.[NAS]
**BRUCE, JOHN,** boatman in Dundee, 1708. [NAS.AC8.100]
**BRUCE, JOHN,** writer in Dundee, testament, 1760, C.B. [NAS]

# THE PEOPLE OF DUNDEE, 1700-1799

**BRUCE, ROBERT,** jr., b. 1724, merchant in Dundee, d. 1748. [HMI]

**BRYDIE, ANDREW,** carpenter in Dundee, 1740. [NAS.AC11.130]

**BRYMER, THOMAS,** late chaise hirer in Dundee, testament, 1771, C.B. [NAS]

**BURGH, ISOBEL,** relict of James Lyon merchant in Dundee, testament, 1726, C.B. [NAS]

**BURGH, JAMES,** mariner in Dundee, & his spouse Catherine Fairnie, testament, 1704, C.B. [NAS]

**BURN, GEORGE,** merchant in Dundee, 1747; testament, 1781, C.B. [NAS.AC11.176]

**BURTON, JAMES,** Excise officer in Dundee, testament, 1715, C.B. [NAS]

**BUTTER, THOMAS,** b.1746, merchant at West Port, Dundee, d.1825, wife Janet McIntosh, b.1745, d. 1818. [HMI]

**CABEL, JAMES,** b. 1741, skipper in Dundee, d. 1814. [HMI]

**CAITHNESS, JOHN,** skipper in Dundee, testament, 1768, C.B.

**CAMPBELL, ALEXANDER,** merchant in Dundee, testament, 1765, C.B. [NAS]

**CAMPBELL, COLIN,** in Dundee, then tenant in the Mains of Dudhope, testament, 1723, 1734, 1737, C.B. [NAS]

**CAMPBELL, WILLIAM,** wright in Dundee, 1748. [NAS.E326.1.50]

**CARMICHAEL, GERSHAM,** minister in Dundee, testament, 1762, C.B. [NAS]

**CARMICHAEL, JOHN,** skipper in Dundee, 1715. [NAS.RD2.105.272]

**CARMICHAEL, WILLIAM,** gardener in Dundee, 1748. [NAS.E326.1.50]

**CARNEGIE, ALEXANDER,** merchant in Dundee, & spouse Isobel Stratton, testament, 1700, C.B. [NAS]

**CARNEGIE, ALISON,** in Dundee, 1748. [NAS.E326.1.50]

**CATHCART, ALEXANDER,** merchant in Dundee, 1701. [NAS.RD2.85.16]

**CATHRO, JAMES,** b. 1735, brewer in Dundee, 1799, d. 1816, wife Elisabeth Patullo, b. 1735, d. 1807. [DCA.B19.3.27/233][HMI]

**CAY, DAVID,** merchant in Dundee, testament, 1783, C.B. [NAS]

# THE PEOPLE OF DUNDEE, 1700-1799

**CHALMERS, JAMES,** master of the Betty of Dundee, 1718. [NAS.CE52.1.3]

**CHALMERS, WILLIAM,** b. 1733, baker in Dundee, d. 1785. [HMI]

**CHAPMAN, JOHN,** weaver in Dundee, 1748. [NAS.E326.1.50]

**CHARTERS, THOMAS,** skipper in Dundee, 1738, master of the Margaret of Dundee, 1739. [NAS.AC10.254; AC11.114]

**CHRISTIE, ANDREW,** cordiner burgess of Dundee, testament, 1710, C.B. [NAS]

**CHRISTIE, ROBERT,** convenor of the trades of Dundee, 1715. [NAS.RD2.105.395]

**CHRISTISON, AGNES,** widow of William Pierrie a merchant in Dundee, testament, 1761, C.B. [NAS]

**CHRISTOPHER, WILLIAM,** b.1769, skipper in Dundee, d.1817, wife Mary Gall. [HMI]

**CLEATTON, or CLYTON, JOHN,** master of the Unicorn of Dundee, at Gairloch in 1718. [SIL#82][NAS.AC13.1.208]

**COLVILLE, ALEXANDER,** of Kincardine, Customs controller at Dundee, 1715. [NAS.AC9.540]

**COLVILLE, JOHN,** merchant in Dundee, 1715. [NAS.RD4.116.1246]

**COLVILLE, Miss,** in Dundee, 1748. [NAS.E326.1.50]

**CONSTABLE, DAVID,** flesher in Hilltown, testament, 1709, C.B. [NAS]

**CONSTABLE, DAVID,** vintner in Dundee, testament, 1778, C.B. [NAS]

**CONSTABLE, JOHN,** flesher in Dundee, 1734. [NAS.AC8.503]

**CONSTABLE, ROBERT,** flesher burgess of Dundee, testament, 1713, C.B.; & his sons John & Thomas, both fleshers there, 1715. [NAS.RD3.144.169]

**COOK, ANDREW,** merchant in Dundee & part-owner of the James of Dundee, 1716. [NAS.AC9.565]

**COOK, ANDREW,** in Dundee, 1748. [NAS.E326.1.50]

**COOK, ELISABETH,** b. 1721, d. 1795, wife of David Smart a baker in Dundee. [HMI]

**COOK, JOHN,** workman in Dundee, 1745. [JA]

**COOK, THOMAS,** b. 1709, flesher in Dundee, d. 1769. [HMI]

**CORSAR, FREDERICK,** merchant in Dundee, 1701; testament, 1742, C.B. [NAS.RD2.85.60]

# THE PEOPLE OF DUNDEE, 1700-1799

**CORSAR, PATRICK,** pinmaker & merchant in Dundee, testament, 1709, C.B. [NAS]
**COUPAR, ALEXANDER,** merchant in the West Port, Dundee, 1751. [DCA.B19.3.27/253]
**COUPAR, GILBERT,** vintner & bailie of Dundee, testament, 1732, C.B. [NAS]
**COUPAR, JOHN,** tailor in Dundee, wife Grizall Lamb, b.1725, d.1754. [HMI]
**COUPAR, PETER,** mariner in Dundee, testament, 1776, C.B.
**COUPAR, WILLIAM,** in Dundee, 1748, testament, 1769, C.B. [NAS.E326.1.50]
**COWAN, ALEXANDER,** maltman in Dundee, & spouse Katherine Shear, testament, 1716, C.B. [NAS]
**COWAN, ALEXANDER,** maltman of Dundee, deceased by 1798. [DCA.B19.3.27/4]
**COWAN, THOMAS,** b. 1724, baker, d. 1807, spouse Janet Millar, b. 1717, d. 1792. [HMI]
**COWAY, JAMES,** merchant in Dundee, 1748. [NAS.E326.1.50]
**COWIE, JAMES,** postmaster in Dundee, testament, 1778, C.B.
**CRABB, THOMAS,** b.1741, d.1799, wife Jean Mackay, b.1731, d.1785. [HMI]
**CRAIK, JOHN,** porter in Dundee, 1798. [DCA.B19.3.27/4]
**CRAMOND, GEORGE,** maltman in Dundee, testament, 1786, C.B. [NAS]
**CRAMOND, JAMES,** d. 1773, wife Helen Matthew, d. 1786. [HMI]
**CRAWFORD, HENRY,** merchant in Dundee, 1703, 1711. [NAS.AC9.26/378]
**CRAWFORD, JAMES,** b.1723, merchant in Dundee, d.1783, wife Helen Coutts, b.1724, d.1806, testament, 1784, 1785, C.B. [NAS][HMI]
**CRAWFORD, Mrs,** in Dundee, 1748. [NAS.E326.1.50]
**CRIGHTON, ALEXANDER,** workman in Dundee, 1745. [JA]
**CRICHTON, ALEXANDER,** b. 1729, maltman in Dundee, d. 1782, wife Margaret Aimer, b. 1731, d. 1782. [HMI]
**CRIGHTON, DAVID,** in Dundee, 1745. [JA]
**CRICHTON, GEORGE,** brewer in Dundee, 1748. [NAS.E326.1.50]
**CRICHTON, GILBERT,** mariner in Dundee, testament, 1713, 1718, C.B. [NAS]

# THE PEOPLE OF DUNDEE, 1700-1799

CRICHTON, JAMES, skipper in Dundee, testament, 1721, C.B.
CRICHTON, JAMES, mariner of Dundee, 1727.
    [NAS.AC8.358]
CRICHTON, JAMES, merchant in Dundee, son of Thomas Crichton a merchant there, testament, 1779, C.B. [NAS]
CRICHTON, JANET, relict of George Moncur maltman in Dundee, testament, 1774, 1777, C.B. [NAS]
CRICHTON, JEAN, relict of William Keillor tailor in Hilltown, testament, 1730, C.B. [NAS]
CRICHTON, JOHN, merchant & bailie of Dundee, 1736, 1748. [NAS.AC10.226; E326.1.50]
CRICHTON, JOHN, sailor in Dundee, 1745. [JA]
CRICHTON, PATRICK, mariner in Dundee, 1716; shipmaster there, testament, 1728, C.B.[NAS.AC9.563]
CRICHTON, PATRICK, b.1713,writer in Dundee, d. 1788. [HMI]
CRIGHTON, THOMAS, surgeon in Dundee, 1745. [JA]
CRICHTON, THOMAS, b. 1712, d. 1791, merchant & bailie of Dundee, testament, 1792, C.B. [NAS][HMI]
CRICHTON, WILLIAM, maltman in Dundee, testament, 1769, 1781, C.B. [NAS]
CRAW, ANDREW, mason in Dundee, 1745. [JA]
CRAW, JAMES, mason in Dundee, 1745. [JA]
CROCKAT, GEORGE, MD in Dundee, testament, 1721, C.B.
CROCKETT, JOHN, merchant Dundee, 1721[NAS.AC9.753]
CROWLE, ANDREW, weaver in Dundee, 1748. [NAS.E326.1.50]
CURRANCE, DAVID, white-iron smith in Dundee, 1799. [DCA.B19.3.27/175/178]
CURRIER, THOMAS, gardener in Dundee, testament, 1728, C.B. [NAS]
DAKERS, WILLIAM, wright in Dundee, testament, 1738, C.B.
DALGLISH, JAMES, labourer in Dundee, 1745. [JA]
DAVIDSON, ALEXANDER, merchant in Dundee, testament, 1729, C.B. [NAS]
DAVIDSON, ANN, relict of James Byack carter in Hilltown, testament, 1785, C.B. [NAS]
DAVIDSON, CHRISTIAN, relict of William Ogilvie teacher at Dundee Grammar School, testament, 1752, C.B. [NAS]

THE PEOPLE OF DUNDEE, 1700-1799

**DAVIDSON, DAVID,** skipper in Dundee, in Murraygate, 1798. [DCA.B19.3.27/14]
**DAVIDSON, JAMES,** master of the Margaret of Dundee, 1734. [NAS.AC8.487]
**DAVIDSON, JOHN,** merchant in Dundee, 1734, 1748. [NAS.AC8.487; E326.1.50]
**DAVIDSON, RICHARD,** merchant in Dundee, 1725. [NAS.AC9.910]
**DAVIDSON, THOMAS,** merchant in Dundee, testament, 1707, C.B. [NAS]
**DAVIDSON, Reverend THOMAS,** in Dundee, 1748. [NAS.E326.1.50]
**DAVIDSON, THOMAS,** writer in Dundee, 1788. [NRAS.124.4.2.56]
**DAVIDSON, WILLIAM,** silversmith in Dundee, 1745. [JA]
**DEANS, ISABEL,** relict of John Davidson merchant in Dundee, testament, 1723, C.B. [NAS]
**DEMPSTER, GEORGE,** merchant of Dundee, 1714, 1715, 1727, 1730, 1744, 1748. [NAS.RD3.97.136; NRAS.244, ms2778/17.4.51; AC9.540; AC8.413/648; E326.1.50]
**DEMPSTER, JOHN,** of Dunnichen, in Dundee, 1748. [NAS.E326.1.50]
**DEMPSTER, WILLIAM,** carpenter in Dundee, 1715. [NAS.RD3.145.354]
**DICK, JAMES,** eldest son of James Dick, writer in Dundee, testament, 1742, C.B. [NAS]
**DICK, JAMES,** b. 1720, merchant in Dundee & Collector of the Cess, d. 1808, wife Christina Wardroper, b. 1728, d. 1793. [HMI]
**DICK, JOHN,** of Pitcarro, in Dundee, 1748. [NAS.E326.1.50]
**DICK, JOHN,** brewer in Dundee, 1748. [NAS.E326.1.50]
**DICK, MUNGO,** in Dundee, 1748. [NAS.E326.1.50]
**DICK, THOMAS,** b. 1739, d. 1787, wife Ann Nairn, b. 1731, d. 1816. [HMI]
**DOBIE, THOMAS,** merchant in Dundee, testament, 1739, C.B.
**DOBIE, THOMAS,** merchant in Dundee, testament, 1764, C.B.
**DOIG, ANDREW,** manufacturer, wife Janet Phillips, b. 1755, d.1785. [HMI]
**DOIG, ARCHIBALD,** merchant in Dundee, 1737, 1748, testament, 1753, C.B. [NAS.AC9.1384; E326.1.50]

# THE PEOPLE OF DUNDEE, 1700-1799

**DOIG, JAMES,** merchant in Dundee, 1749, testament, 1758, C.B. [NAS.AC8.715]
**DOIG, JAMES,** merchant in Dundee, invoices, 1796-1809. [NAS.CS96.1605]
**DOIG, JANET,** relict of Henry Watson hammerman in Dundee, testament, 1772, C.B. [NAS]
**DOIG, JOHN,** maltman in Dundee, d.1763. [HMI]
**DOIG, MARGARET,** b. 1697, d. 1741. [HMI]
**DOIG, ROBERT,** b. 1736, manufacturer in Dundee, d. 1802, wife Margaret Cock, d. 1778. [HMI]
**DOIG, WILLIAM,** hammerman in Dundee, wife Margaret Allison, around 1790. [HMI]
**DON, PATRICK,** chapman in Dundee, testament, 1737, C.B.
**DONALDSON, DAVID,** maltman in Dundee, testament, 1724, C.B. [NAS]
**DONALDSON, JOHN,** merchant in Dundee, deed, 1714. [NAS.RD3.97.136]
**DONALDSON, JOHN,** of Invereighty, in Dundee, dead by 1748. [NAS.E326.1.50]
**DONALDSON, THOMAS,** mason in Dundee, testament, 1775, C.B. [NAS]
**DONALDSON, WILLIAM,** skipper burgess of Dundee, 1706, 1710, testament, 1714, C.B. [NAS.AC9.238; AC9.359]
**DONALDSON, WILLIAM,** merchant in Dundee, deed, 1714. [NAS.RD3.97.136]
**DOOLY, ARCHIBALD,** physician in Dundee, testament, 1767, C.B.. [NAS]
**DORWARD, ROBERT,** shoemaker in Blackscroft, Dundee, 1799. [DCA.B19.3.27/268]
**DOUGLAS, JOHN,** labourer from Dundee, emigrated via Kirkcaldy to Brunswick, North Carolina, aboard the Jamaica Packet of Burntisland in June 1775. [NA.T47.12]
**DOUGLAS, THOMAS,** wright in Dundee, 1706. [NAS.AC8.65]
**DOURE, JOHN,** skipper in Dundee, 1708. [NAS.AC8.100]
**DOVE, JAMES,** mariner in Dundee, 1725. [NAS.AC9.924]
**DOWIE, JOHN,** skipper in Dundee, 1711, testament, 1721, C.B. [NAS.AC9.406]
**DOWIE, Captain ROBERT,** skipper in Dundee, testament, 1729, C.B. [NAS]

# THE PEOPLE OF DUNDEE, 1700-1799

**DOWIE, THOMAS,** merchant & bailie of Dundee, 1757. [NRAS.150.3.24]

**DRON, JOHN,** b.1737, a sawyer, d.1810, wife Margaret Keith. [HMI]

**DRUMMOND, JAMES,** skipper in Dundee, testament, 1798, 1799, C.B. [NAS]

**DRUMMOND, JOHN,** mariner in Dundee, spouse Agnes Ramsay, 1774. [NAS.CS16.1.157/399]

**DRUMMOND, WILLIAM,** tailor in Dundee, testament, 1704, 1707, 1708, 1713, C.B. [NAS]

**DUFF, ALEXANDER,** apprentice in Dundee, 1745. [JA]

**DUFF, PETER,** shipmaster in Dundee, testament, 1785, C.B.

**DUFF, ROBERT,** in Dundee, 1796. [DCA.B19.3.26/6]

**DUFFIE, JAMES,** merchant in Dundee, & Collector to the Guildry there, testament, 1706, C.B.. [NAS]

**DUFFUS, JAMES,** dead by 1748, in Dundee, 1748. [NAS.E326.1.50]

**DUKE, WILLIAM,** mariner in Dundee, 1714. [NAS.AC11.12]

**DUKE, WILLIAM,** merchant in Dundee, 1714. [NAS.AC11.12]

**DUNBAR, DAVID,** b.1680, merchant in Dundee,d.1723, testament, 1728, C.B. [HMI]

**DUNCAN, AGNES,** spouse to James Milne a merchant in Dundee, testament, 1777, C.B. [NAS]

**DUNCAN, ALEXANDER,** late provost of Dundee, testament, 1731, C.B. [NAS]

**DUNCAN, ALEXANDER,** of Lundie, in Dundee, 1748. [NAS.E326.1.50]

**DUNCAN, ALEXANDER,** clerk of Dundee, 1748, testament, 1757, C.B. [NAS.E326.1.50]

**DUNCAN, DAVID,** master of the Margaret of Dundee, 1730, father of John, Helen, Margaret, George & Agnes, 1734; testament, 1747, C.B. [NAS.AC8.413/500]

**DUNCAN, GEORGE,** town clerk of Dundee, testament, 1723, 1724, 1730, C.B. [NAS]

**DUNCAN, ISOBEL,** widow of Provost Patrick Yeaman a merchant in Dundee, testament, 1772, 1776, C.B.. [NAS]

**DUNCAN, JAMES,** mariner in Dundee, testament, 1707, C.B.

**DUNCAN, JAMES,** late Convenor of the Trades in Dundee, testament, 1784, C.B. [NAS]

# THE PEOPLE OF DUNDEE, 1700-1799

**DUNCAN, JAMES,** grain & linen merchant in Dundee, 1790s. [NAS.CS96.81]
**DUNCAN, JANET,** widow of George Lyon merchant bailie of Dundee, testament, 1750, C.B. [NAS]
**DUNCAN, JANET,** widow of Leonard Robertson shipmaster in Dundee, & of David Balvaird a merchant in Dundee, testament, 1773, C.B. [NAS]
**DUNCAN, JOHN,** apprentice carpenter in Dundee, 1745. [JA]
**DUNCAN, PETER,** workman in Dundee, 1745. [JA]
**DUNCAN, WILLIAM,** b.1703, maltman, d.1743, wife Elizabeth Dall. [HMI]
**DUNCAN, WILLIAM,** brewer in Dundee, 1748. [NAS.E326.1.50]
**DURHAM, ELIZABETH,** widow of George Lindsay, in Dundee, testament, 1755, C.B. [NAS]
**DURHAM, Mrs,** in Dundee, 1748. [NAS.E326.1.50]
**EASSON, ROBERT,** b. 1736, d. 1810. [HMI]
**EDWARDS, DAVID,** b. 1768, vintner in Dundee, d. 1819. [HMI]
**ELDER, WILLIAM,** b. 1731, d. 1804, wife Jean Gregor, b. 1740, d. 1802. [HMI]
**FAICHNEY, PATRICK,** in Millshades later in Hawkhill, testament, 1797, C.B. [NAS]
**FAIRWEATHER, JAMES,** b.1670, merchant & provost of Dundee, 1714, testament, 1738, CB. [NAS.RD4.89.550]
**FAIRWEATHER, JAMES,** master of the Ann & Isabel of Dundee, 1717, skipper in Dundee, 1748. [NAS.CE52.1.3; E326.1.50]
**FAIRWEATHER, JAMES,** sailcloth manufacturer in Dundee, books, 1779-1785. [NAS.CS96.1641]
**FAIRWEATHER, JAMES,** merchant trading between Dundee & Carolina, 1773; testament, 1787, C.B. [NAS.E504.11.7/8]
**FAIRWEATHER, JOHN,** b.1706, merchant & bailie of Dundee, 1746, 1748; d.1760; testament, 1771, C.B. [NAS.AC8.679; E326.1.50][HMI]
**FAIRWEATHER, THOMAS,** merchant & bailie of Dundee, 1703, 1714; testament, 1730, C.B. [NAS.AC9.40; RD4.89.625]
**FALCONER, Dr WILLIAM,** of Peebles, resident in Dundee, testament, 1768, C.B. [NAS]

# THE PEOPLE OF DUNDEE, 1700-1799

**FARMER, JOHN,** in Dundee, testament, 1752, C.B. [NAS]
**FARQUHAR, JOHN,** land-waiter in Dundee, testament, 1731, C.B. [NAS]
**FARQUHARSON, CHARLES,** b. 1708, watchmaker in Dundee, d. 1788. [HMI]
**FARQUHARSON, PAUL,** in Dundee, 1748. [NAS.E326.1.50]
**FENTON, JOHN,** b. 1841, dyer in Dundee, d. 1827, husband of Elisabeth Adamson, b. 1763, d. 1835. [HMI]
**FENTON, THOMAS,** servant in Dundee, 1745. [JA]
**FERGUSON, ANDREW,** merchant & bailie in Dundee, 1748, testament, 1770, C.B. [NAS.E326.1.50]
**FERGUSON, JAMES,** maltman burgess of Dundee, testament, 1729, C.B. [NAS]
**FERGUSON, JOHN,** b. 1710, merchant in Dundee, d. 1770, spouse of Margaret Ramsay, b. 1721, d. 1781. [HMI]
**FERGUSON, JOSEPH,** weaver in Chapel of Keillor, Dundee, 1745. [JA]
**FERRIER, ALEXANDER,** minister in Dundee, testament, 1769, C.B. [NAS]
**FINLAY, ALEXANDER,** b.1750, skipper in Dundee, d.1826, wife Margaret Kidd, b.1753, d.1834. [HMI]
**FINDLAY, ANDREW,** mason in Dundee, 1706. [NAS.AC8.65]
**FINDLAY, ROBERT,** master of the Janet of Dundee, 1750; testament, 1765, C.B. [NAS.AC11.189]
**FLETCHER, DAVID,** skipper in Dundee, 1712. [NAS.AC9.427]
**FLETCHER, JAMES,** merchant in Dundee, 1714. [NAS.RD2.85.301]
**FLETCHER, Mrs,** in Dundee, 1748. [NAS.E326.1.50]
**FORBES, PETER,** b. 1741, d. 1796. [HMI]
**FORD, DAVID,** merchant in Dundee, testament, 1783, C.B.
**FORRESTER, MARGARET,** daughter of the late John Forrester surgeon apothecary in Dundee, testament, 1775, C.B.
**FORRESTER, MARTIN,** in Dundee, 1731. [NAS.AC8.434]
**FOTHERINGHAM, AGNES,** daughter of the late Dr David Fotheringham a physician in Dundee,1748, testament, 1751, C.B. [NAS.E326.1.50]
**FOTHERINGHAM, Dr DAVID,** physician in Dundee, testament, 1744, C.B. [NAS]
**FOTHERINGHAM, DAVID,** merchant in Dundee, 1745. [JA]

# THE PEOPLE OF DUNDEE, 1700-1799

**FOTHERINGHAM, HELEN,** daughter of the late Dr David Fotheringham physician in Dundee, testament, 1792, C.B.
**FOTHERINGHAM, JAMES,** merchant in Dundee, 1748; testament, 1759, 1760, C.B. [NAS.E326.1.50]
**FOTHERINGHAM, JAMES,** merchant trading between Dundee & South Carolina, 1770. [NAS.E504.11.7]
**FOTHERINGHAM, Dr ROBERT,** physician in Dundee, testament, 1762, C.B. [NAS]
**FOULLAR, DAVID,** mariner in Dundee, testament, 1718, C.B.
**FULLERTON, GEORGE,** merchant in Dundee, testament, 1772, C.B. [NAS]
**FYFE, DAVID,** merchant in Dundee, testament, 1728, C.B.
**FIFE, DAVID,** in Dundee, 1748. [NAS.E326.1.50]
**FYFFE, DAVID,** in Dundee, late of Jamaica, 1781. [NAS.RS35.39]
**FYFFE, GEORGE,** merchant in Dundee, testament, 1767, C.B.
**FIFE, JAMES,** of Dron, in Dundee, 1748. [NAS.E326.1.50]
**FYFFE, THOMAS,** sailor in Dundee, testament, 1782, C.B.
**GAIRNS, DAVID,** of Lattine, in Dundee, 1748. [NAS.E326.1.50]
**GALL, ALEXANDER,** merchant in Dundee, 1729, 1735. [NAS.AC9.1067; AC11.84]
**GALLATLY, Reverend JOHN,** in Dundee, 1748. [NAS.E326.1.50]
**GALLOWAY, DAVID,** merchant in Dundee, 1798. [DCA.B19.3.27/1]
**GALLOWAY, HARRY,** Customs clerk in Dundee, testament, 1751, C.B. [NAS]
**GALLOWAY, JANET,** in Dundee, testament, 1794, C.B. [NAS]
**GALLOWAY, JOHN,** flaxdresser in Chapelshade, 1796, wife Margaret Duncan, b. 1772, d. 1795. [HMI]
**GALLOWAY, WILLIAM,** merchant in Dundee, testament, 1772, 1773, C.B. [NAS]
**GARDEN, CHRISTIAN,** relict of Patrick Smith litster in Dundee, testament, 1766, C.B. [NAS]
**GARDEN, JAMES,** bonnetmaker on the Hill of Dundee, 1706. [NAS.AC9.216]
**GARDEN, MAGDALEN,** daughter of the late Andrew Garden litster, testament, 1766, C.B. [NAS]
**GARDEN, ROBERT,** maltmaker in Dundee, 1706. [NAS.AC9.216]

# THE PEOPLE OF DUNDEE, 1700-1799

**GARDINER, ANDREW,** wright in Dundee, 1720. [NAS.B59.24.11.150]

**GARDYNE, ISABEL,** widow of James Smyton merchant in Dundee, testament, 1735, C.B. [NAS]

**GARDYNE, JAMES,** son of the late Andrew Gardyne, in Clepington, testament, 1722, C.B. [NAS]

**GARDYNE, ROBERT,** merchant in Dundee, testament, 1716, C.B. [NAS]

**GARLAND, DAVID,** b. 1694, wright in Dundee, d.1772, spouse Jean Munro, b.1712, d.1784. [HMI]

**GARVIE, THOMAS,** mariner in Dundee, testament, 1719, C.B.

**GAVEN, PETER,** b.1725, skipper in Dundee, d.1758, wife Janet Watson, b.1737, d.1763. [HMI]

**GEAREY, GEORGE,** merchant in Dundee, testament, 1766, C.B. [NAS]

**GEIGIE, GEORGE,** weaver in Dundee, 1745. [JA]

**GEIKIE, ALEXANDER,** maltman in Dundee, testament, 1721, C.B. [NAS]

**GEIKIE, DAVID,** maltman in Dundee, wife (1) Isobel Crichton, b.1683, d.1714; (2) Margaret Cardean, b.1691, d.1730. [HMI]

**GEIKIE, HENRY,** merchant & Provost of Dundee, testament, 1792, C.B. [NAS]

**GEIKIE, THOMAS,** cordiner in Dundee, testament, 1740, C.B.

**GIBB, Deacon ALEXANDER,** in Dundee, 1748. [NAS.E326.1.50]

**GIBB, ALEXANDER,** flesher in Dundee, testament, 1771, C.B.

**GIBB, DAVID,** flesher in Dundee, testament, 1775, 1776, C.B.

**GIBB, JAMES,** bonnet maker in Dundee, testament, 1722, C.B.

**GIBB, JAMES,** sailor in Dundee, 1745. [JA]

**GIBB, JAMES,** salt/corn measurer in Dundee, testament, 1754, C.B. [NAS]

**GIBB, JOHN,** Convenor in Dundee, 1748. [NAS.E326.1.50]

**GIBB, WILLIAM,** maltman in Dundee, 1725. [NAS.AC9.943]

**GIBSON, DAVID,** porter in Dundee, 1745. [JA]

**GIBSON, JOHN,** weaver in Dundee, 1745. [JA]

**GIBSON, WILLIAM,** cooper in Dundee, testament, 1755, C.B.

**GILLIES, THOMAS,** maltman in Dundee, 1714. [NAS.RD2.85.301]

# THE PEOPLE OF DUNDEE, 1700-1799

**GLASS, Reverend JOHN,** in Dundee, a letter, 1745; 1748. [NAS.B59.24.1.27; E326.1.50]
**GLASS, THOMAS,** merchant in Dundee, 1748, bookseller in Dundee, testament, 1763, C.B. [NAS.E326.1.50]
**GLEIG, JAMES,** in Dundee, 1725. [NAS.AC9.943]
**GOLDMAN, BARBARA & MARGARET,** daughters of the late Alexander Goldman a merchant in Dundee, testament, 1777, C.B. [NAS]
**GOLDMAN, JOHN,** merchant in Dundee, relict Euphan Smith, 1714. [NAS.RD3.95.112]
**GOLLON, GEORGE,** writer in Dundee, testament, 1737, C.B.
**GOURLAY, Deacon JAMES,** in Dundee, 1748. [NAS.E326.1.50]
**GOURLAY, JAMES,** sometime merchant in Dundee, only son of the late John Gourlay glover there, 1798.. [DCA.B19.3.27/15]
**GOURLAY, JOHN,** merchant in Dundee then in Carolina, 1740. [NAS.CS16.1.69]
**GOURLAY, JOHN,** glover in Dundee, testament, 1742, C.B.
**GOURLAY, WILLIAM,** maltman burgess of Dundee, testament, 1710, C.B. [NAS]
**GOWANS, WILLIAM,** b.1725, d.1797, wife Elizabeth Mustard, b.1729, d.1767. [HMI]
**GRAHAM, ALEXANDER,** merchant in Dundee, testament, 1725, C.B. [NAS]
**GRAHAM, ALEXANDER,** merchant in Dundee,1736, 1745. [NAS.RS35.15.246][JA]
**GRAHAM, ALEXANDER,** writer in Dundee, 1745. [JA]
**GRAHAM, ALEXANDER,** of Duntrune, in Dundee, 1748. [NAS.E326.1.50]
**GRAHAM, DAVID,** vintner in Dundee, & wife Margaret Rodger, testament, 1725, C.B. [NAS]
**GRAHAM, DAVID,** merchant in Dundee, 1745. [JA]
**GRAHAM, DAVID,** son of the late John Graham merchant in Dundee, testament, 1750, C.B. [NAS]
**GRAHAM, ELIZABETH,** relict of Captain Alexander Stewart shipmaster in Dundee, testament, 1776, C.B. [NAS]
**GRAHAM, GRIZEL,** daughter of the late John Graham sr., merchant & bailie of Dundee, testament, 1760, 1767, C.B.
**GRAHAM, JAMES,** merchant in Dundee, testament, 1718, C.B.

# THE PEOPLE OF DUNDEE, 1700-1799

**GRAHAM, JAMES,** merchant in Dundee, sasine, 1757. [NAS.RS35.18.259]
**GRAHAM, JANET,** relict of John Tindal writer in Dundee, testament, 1773, C.B. [NAS]
**GRAHAM, JOHN,** merchant in Dundee, 1705; late bailie of Dundee, 1710. [NAS.AC13.1.32; AC8.123; AC9.359]
**GRAHAM, JOHN,** merchant in Dundee, & Grizel, daughter of the late David Graham of Fintry, marriage contract, 1736; testament, 1771, C.B. [NRAS.2148.14.52]
**GRAHAM, JOHN,** mariner in Dundee, eldest son of the late Walter Graham a merchant there, testament, 1771, C.B.
**GRAHAM, MARGARET,** relict of Thomas Pearson a maltman in Dundee, testament, 1720, C.B. [NAS]
**GRAHAM, MARJORIE,** wife of John Forrester of Milnhill, a sasine, 1730. [NRAS.2201.2.5]
**GRAHAM, ROBERT,** merchant in Dundee, testament, 1761, C.B. [NAS]
**GRAHAM, WALTER,** eldest son of the late James Graham a merchant in Dundee, testament, 1718, C.B. [NAS]
**GRAHAM, WILLIAM,** merchant in Edinburgh later in Dundee, testament, 1773, C.B. [NAS]
**GRANT, WILLIAM,** mariner in Dundee, testament, 1743, C.B.
**GRAY, DAVID,** servant in Dundee, 1745. [JA]
**GRAY, JAMES,** merchant in Dundee, testament, 1724, C.B.
**GRAY, JAMES,** b. 1762, merchant in Dundee, 1794, d. 1826. [DCA.B19.3.27/210][HMI]
**GRAY, JOHN,** merchant in Dundee, 1714. [NAS.RD4.88.359]
**GRAY, PATRICK,** surgeon in Dundee, 1748. [NAS.E326.1.50]
**GRAY, PETER,** in Dundee, dead by 1748. [NAS.E326.1.50]
**GRAY, ROBERT,** skipper of Dundee, 1706. [NAS.AC8.65]
**GRAY, ROBERT,** keeper of the Tolbooth of Dundee, 1798.. [DCA.B19.3.27/5]
**GREENHILL, ALEXANDER,** merchant in Dundee, curator for Robert Fletcher of Ballinshoe, 1787. [NRAS.124.4.2]
**GREENHILL, CATHERINE,** b. 1716, d. 1790. [HMI]
**GREENHILL, CHRISTIAN,** b.1716, d. 1800. [HMI]
**GREENHILL, JEAN,** b.1725, d. 1703. [HMI]
**GREENHILL, MARGARET,** b. 1728, d. 1804. [HMI]
**GREENHILL, MARY,** b.1772, d. 1794. [HMI]

# THE PEOPLE OF DUNDEE, 1700-1799

**GREENHILL, PATRICK,** b.1723, d. 1792, & daughter Margaret, b. 1772, d. 1794. [HMI]
**GREGORY, JOHN,** land-waiter in Dundee, testament, 1783, C.B. [NAS]
**GREGORY, WILLIAM,** skipper of Dundee, 1704. [NAS.AC8.30]
**GREIG, DAVID,** master of the Agnes of Dundee, a bark, from Leith to Wick in 1734. [SIL#379]
**GREIG, ELIZABETH,** teacher in Dundee, 1788. [NAS.B59.24.6.83]
**GREIG, THOMAS,** carpenter in Dundee, testament, 1780, C.B.
**GREIVE, GEORGE,** merchant in Dundee, testament, 1751, C.B.
**GREIVE, JAMES,** surgeon apothecary in Dundee, testament, 1729, 1737, C.B. [NAS]
**GRUB, WILLIAM,** mariner in Dundee, testament, 1743, C.B.
**GUILD, ALEXANDER,** maltman in Dundee, testament, 1768, C.B. [NAS]
**GUILD, ALEXANDER,** baker in Dundee, 1780s. [HMI]
**GUILD, JAMES,** b.1715, maltman in Dundee, 1748, d.1782, wife Jean Lindsay, b.1721, d.1776. [NAS.E326.1.50][HMI]
**GUILD, JOHN,** b.1742, chief magistrate of Dundee, d.1819, wife Catherine Jamieson, b.1746, d.1823. [HMI]
**GUILLAN, DAVID,** brewer in Dundee, 1798. [DCA.B19.3.27/1]
**GUTHRIE, ALEXANDER,** merchant in Dundee, 1748. [NAS.E326.1.50]
**GUTHRIE, ALEXANDER,** Cess collector in Dundee, testament 1776, C.B. [NAS]
**GUTHRIE, ANNE,** in Dundee, testament, 1760, C.B. [NAS]
**GUTHRIE, DAVID,** apothecary in Dundee, relict Matilda Adam, 1715. [NAS.RD3.145.158]
**GUTHRIE, CHARLES,** maltman in Dundee, 1772. [NAS.CH2.2118.67][HMI]
**GUTHRIE, GILBERT,** merchant in Dundee, spouse of Ann Guthrie, testament, 1718, C.B. [NAS]
**GUTHRIE, HENRY,** a merchant in Dundee, 1709. [NAS.AC9.337]
**GUTHRIE, JAMES,** bailie of Dundee, deceased, father of John, James, Robert, Thomas, William, Alexander & Henry, 1718. [NAS.AC13.1.211]

# THE PEOPLE OF DUNDEE, 1700-1799

**GUTHRIE, JAMES,** of Craigie, in Dundee, 1748. [NAS.E326.1.50]

**GUTHRIE, JOHN,** b. 1739, a merchant in Dundee, d. 1786, testament, 1786, C.B.; wife Helen Yeaman, b. 1755, d. 1818. [HMI]

**GUTHRIE, JOHN,** in Hilltown, son of John Guthrie, 1798. [DCA.B19.3.27/181]

**GUTHRIE, ROBERT,** merchant in Dundee, 1745, 1748. [JA][NAS.E326.1.50]

**GUTHRIE, THOMAS,** merchant in Dundee, testament, 1795, C.B. [NAS]

**GUTHRIE, THOMAS,** b.1736, merchant in Dundee, d.1813, wife Jean Pyot, b.1738, d.1806. [HMI]

**GUTHRIE, WILLIAM,** of Clepington, in Dundee, 1748. [NAS.E326.1.50]

**GUTHRIE, Miss,** in Dundee, 1748. [NAS.E326.1.50]

**HACKIE, JOHN,** a weaver in Dundee, 1745. [JA]

**HACKNEY, WILLIAM,** a merchant in Dundee, 1773. [NAS.CS16.1.154/36]

**HALIBURTON, DAVID,** a merchant in Dundee, 1748. [NAS.E326.1.50]

**HALIBURTON, JAMES,** b. 1730, magistrate of Dundee, d.1802. [HMI]

**HALIBURTON, JAMES,** merchant & bailie of Dundee, 1737, 1748. [NAS.AC9.1384; E326.1.50]

**HALIBURTON, JOHN,** master of the William of Dundee, 1705, 1714, 1716, 1730, testament, C.B. [NAS.AC9.136/567; RD4.88.227]

**HALIBURTON, THOMAS,** wright in Dundee, 1745, 1751. [JA][NAS.B59.38.2.253]

**HAMILTON, ANDREW,** b.1680, d. 1729. [HMI]

**HAMILTON, JAMES,** sailor in Dundee, testament, 1757, C.B.

**HAMILTON, ROBERT,** b.1714, mason in Dundee, d.1802, wife Jean Strang, b.1716, d.1773. [HMI]

**HAY, JAMES,** merchant in Dundee, 1737; testament, 1755, C.B. [NAS.AC9.1384]

**HAY, JAMES,** writer in Dundee, testament, 1798, C.B. [NAS]

**HAY, PATRICK,** merchant in Dundee, testament, 1742, 1752, C.B. [NAS]

# THE PEOPLE OF DUNDEE, 1700-1799

**HAZEEL, DAVID,** manufacturer in Dundee, 1799.
[DCA.B19.3.27/233]
**HENDERSON, ALEXANDER,** merchant in Dundee, 1745. [JA]
**HENDERSON, ALEXANDER,** brewer in Dundee, 1748.
[NAS.E326.1.50]
**HENDERSON, FRANCIS,** merchant in Dundee, 1735, 1745, 1748,1749. [JA][NAS.B59.37.13.16; E326.1.50; AC8.718]
**HENDERSON, JAMES,** slater in Dundee, 1745. [JA]
**HENDERSON, MARGARET,** in Dundee, testament, 1757, C.B. [NAS]
**HENDERSON, MARY,** in Dundee, testament, 1775, C.B. [NAS]
**HENDERSON, Dr ROBERT,** b. 1750, physician in Dundee, d. 1824, wife Ann, b. 1759, d. 1808. [HMI]
**HENDERSON, THOMAS,** merchant in Dundee, 1748, testament, 1755. C.B. [NAS.E326.1.50]
**HENDERSON, THOMAS,** weaver in Dundee, testament, 1796, C.B. [NAS]
**HENDERSON, WILLIAM,** slater in Dundee, 1745. [JA]
**HENDERSON, Mrs,** in Dundee, 1748. [NAS.E326.1.50]
**HENRY, ALEXANDER,** dyer in Dundee, 1745. [JA]
**HILL, ABRAM,** b. 1732, d. 1816, wife Effie Mitchell, b. 1728, d. 1811. [HMI]
**HILL, ALEXANDER,** gardener in Dundee, testament, 1791, C.B. [NAS]
**HILL, DAVID,** brewer in Dundee, 1748. [NAS.E326.1.50]
**HILL, JAMES,** b. 1778, weaver in Dundee, who was murdered in Chapelshade in 1799. [HMI]
**HILL, JOHN,** merchant in Dundee, testament, 1747, C.B. [NAS]
**HILL, ROBERT,** b. 1672, a maltman, d. 1745. [HMI]
**HILL, THOMAS,** joiner from Dundee, emigrated via Kirkcaldy to Brunswick, North Carolina, aboard the Jamaica Packet of Burntisland in June 1775. [NA.T47.12]
**HILL, WILLIAM,** skipper in Dundee, testament, 1775, C.B.
**HODGE, Mrs,** in Dundee, 1748. [NAS.E326.1.50]
**HOGG, JOHN,** bonnet maker in Dundee, testament, 1734, C.B.
**HOGG, WILLIAM,** in Dundee, 1748. [NAS.E326.1.50]
**HOOD, FREDERICK,** at West Port of Dundee, testament, 1796, C.B. [NAS]
**HORN, CHARLES,** shoemaker in Dundee, 1745. [JA]
**HORN, JAMES,** brewer in Dundee, 1748. [NAS.E326.1.50]

# THE PEOPLE OF DUNDEE, 1700-1799

**HORN, WILLIAM,** b.1725, weaver in Dundee, d.1773. [HMI]
**HOW, DAVID,** b. 1754, merchant in Dundee, d. 1794, husband of Eliza Doig. [HMI]
**HUNTER, ALEXANDER,** of Balskelly, in Dundee, 1748. [NAS.E326.1.50]
**HUNTER, ANDREW,** merchant in Dundee, 1710. [NAS.AC9.359]
**HUNTER, DAVID,** merchant in Dundee, 1725, 1729. [NAS.AC9.881; AC8.394]
**HUNTER, DAVID,** merchant in Dundee, 1798. [DCA.B19.3.27/4]
**HUNTER, JOHN,** mariner in Dundee, testament, 1731, C.B.
**HUNTER, JOHN,** merchant in Dundee, testament, 1772, C.B.
**HUNTER, PATRICK,** in Dundee, letters, 1776-1782. [NAS.B59.37.4.14/15]
**HUTTON, DAVID,** b.1730, skipper in Dundee, d.1793, wife Isobel Henderson, b.1746, d.1809. [HMI]
**HUTTON, ROBERT,** skipper in Dundee, testament, 1799, C.B.
**IMRIE, DUNCAN,** b. 1754, ship carpenter from Dundee, settled in Carolina & later East Florida, dead by 1782. [NAS.CC8.8.125]
**INGLIS, ROBERT,** master of the <u>Margaret of Dundee</u>, 1716/1721. [NAS.AC8.190; AC9.744]
**IRELAND, JOHN,** skipper in Dundee, testament, 1771, C.B.
**IRONS, DAVID,** shoemaker in Dundee, 1780s. [HMI]
**IRVINE, WILLIAM,** wright in Dundee, testament, 1785, C.B.
**JACK, EUPHAN,** testament, 1737, C.B. [NAS]
**JACK, HENRY,** b.1737, d. 1806, wife Jean Hunter, b. 1741, d. 1830. [HMI]
**JACKSON, ALEXANDER,** merchant in Dundee, spouse Euphemia Duncan, testament, 1707, C.B. [NAS]
**JACKSON, CHARLES,** brewer in Dundee, 1745. [JA]
**JACKSON, JAMES,** testament, 1718, C.B. [NAS]
**JAMIESON, DAVID,** wright in Dundee, testament, 1798, C.B.
**JAMIESON, ELISABETH,** relict of William Gibb a maltman in Dundee, testament, 1746, C.B. [NAS]
**JAMIESON, JAMES,** merchant in Dundee, testament, 1770, C.B. [NAS]
**JAMIESON, JOHN,** shoemaker in Dundee, wife Margaret Leuchars, around 1790. [HMI]

# THE PEOPLE OF DUNDEE, 1700-1799

**JAMIESON, WILLIAM,** a merchant trading between Dundee & Carolina, 1773. [NAS.E504.11.8]
**JAMIESON, Mrs,** in Dundee, 1748. [NAS.E326.1.50]
**JOBSON, ANDREW,** merchant tailor in Dundee, 1799. [DCA.B19.3.27/266]
**JOBSON, DAVID,** writer in Dundee, 1766, testament,1791, C.B.[NAS.CS16.1.125/250][DCA.B19.3.27/11]
**JOBSON, JOHN,** b.1698, merchant & bailie of Dundee, 1734, 1748, 1774, d.1788. [NAS.AC8.500; E326.1.50; NAS.CS16.1.157/399][HMI]
**JOHNSTON, ALEXANDER,** silversmith in Dundee, 1745. [JA]
**JOHNSTON, JAMES,** brewer in Dundee, 1748. [NAS.E326.1.50]
**JOHNSTON, JAMES,** writer in Dundee, testament, 1751, 1758, C.B. [NAS]
**JOHNSTONE, JAMES,** surgeon & provost of Dundee, testament, 1799, C.B. [NAS]
**JOHNSTONE, JAMES,** surgeon HEICS, son of Provost James Johnstone of Dundee, was admitted as a burgess of Dundee, in 1799. [DCA: Dundee Burgess Register]
**JOHNSTON, ROBERT,** b.1755, d.1806, wife Agnes Ross. [HMI]
**KAY, JAMES,** in Dundee, 1748. [NAS.E326.1.50]
**KAY, JAMES,** merchant in Dundee, 1748. [NAS.E326.1.50]
**KAY, WILLIAM,** wright in Dundee, 1748. [NAS.E326.1.50]
**KEAY, DAVID,** b. 1725, a skipper in Dundee, d. 1807, spouse Susanna Bower, b. 1744, d. 1805. [HMI]
**KEILLER, MUNGO,** porter in Dundee, 1796. [DCA.B19.3.26/1]
**KEILLOR. WILLIAM,** weaver in Hilltown, testament, 1730, C.B. [NAS]
**KEIR, ELSPETH,** b. 1715, d. 1792. [HMI]
**KEITH, ALEXANDER,** music master in Dundee, testament, 1717, C.B. [NAS]
**KESSAN, THOMAS,** merchant in Dundee, 1706. [NAS.AC9.238]
**KEY, DAVID,** tailor in Dundee, testament, 1764, C.B. [NAS]
**KEY, JAMES,** master of the Elizabeth of Dundee, 1737; testament, 1786, C.B. [NAS.AC8.547]
**KIDD, ALEXANDER,** b. 1740, skipper in Dundee, d.1826, wife Helen Guild, b.1746, d.1790. [HMI]

# THE PEOPLE OF DUNDEE, 1700-1799

**KIDD, DAVID,** apprentice town clerk in Dundee, 1799. [DCA.B19.3.27/202]
**KIDD, JOHN,** skipper in Dundee, testament, 1796, C.B. [NAS]
**KIDD, PATRICK,** merchant & vintner in Dundee, 1707, 1714, testament, 1721, C.B. [NAS.AC9.273; RD2.85.266]
**KIDD, RICHARD,** mariner in Dundee, testament, 1783, C.B.
**KIDD, ROBERT,** a mariner in Dundee, testament, 1751, C.B.
**KIDD, Mrs,** in Dundee, dead by 1748. [NAS.E326.1.50]
**KINLOCH, GEORGE,** a merchant in Dundee, & a partner in the Dundee Ropery, 1734; bailie in 1748. [NAS.AC8.503; E326.1.50]
**KINLOCH, JOHN,** of Clesbany, MD in Dundee, testament, 1732, 1734, & 1735, C.B. [NAS]
**KINLOCH, Dr JOHN,** of Clashbinnie, physician in Dundee, testament, 1778, C.B. [NAS]
**KINNAIRD, ANDREW,** maltman in Dundee, 1706. [NAS.AC9.216]
**KINNARIS, Captain GEORGE,** dead by 1748; ?testament, 1735, 1737, 1738, C.B. [NAS.E326.1.50]
**KINNEAR, ROBERT,** b.1721, maltman in Dundee, d. 1772. [HMI]
**KINNEAR, ROBERT,** skipper in Dundee, testament, 1799, C.B.
**KINNER, WILLIAM,** b.1700, d.1769. [HMI]
**KINNIMOND, ALEXANDER,** mason in Dundee, 1745. [JA]
**KINNIMOND, PETER,** writer in Dundee, 1748; testament, 1760, C.B. [NAS.E326.1.50]
**KIRKCALDY, ALISON,** relict of James Birrell a skipper in Dundee, testament, 1776, C.B. [NAS]
**KIRKCALDY, DAVID,** merchant in Dundee, relict Elizabeth Wedderburn, testament, 1768, CB. [NAS]
**KIRKCALDY, DAVID,** merchant in Dundee, & master of the Hospital there, 1798. [DCA.B19.3.27/1]
**KIRKCALDY, Mrs,** in Dundee, 1748. [NAS.E326.1.50]
**KIRKLAND, WILLIAM,** b.1752, veterinary surgeon in Dundee, d.1787, wife Jean Smith, b.1753, d.1805. [HMI]
**KNIGHT, HENRY,** maltman in Dundee, testament, 1751, C.B.
**KNIGHT, JAMES,** skipper in Dundee, testament, 1719, C.B.
**KNIGHT, JAMES,** baker in Dundee, 1748. [NAS.E326.1.50]
**KYD, PATRICK,** merchant in Dundee, 1719. [NAS.SC20.33.9]

# THE PEOPLE OF DUNDEE, 1700-1799

**LAIRD, ANDREW**, b. 1704, a merchant in Dundee, d. 1780, husband of Ann Graham, b. 1702, d. 1769. [JA][HMI][NAS.E326.1.50]

**LAMB, WILLIAM**, merchant in Dundee, testament, 1761, C.B.

**LAMY, SYLVESTER**, Customs officer at Dundee, 1736. [NAS.AC10.231]

**LATIMER, CHRISTOPHER**, Excise officer in Dundee, husband of Elizabeth Wardroper, 1770. [NAS.CS16.1.141/190]

**LAWSON, JAMES**, b.1743, d.1792, wife Margaret Milne, b.1741, d.1792. [HMI]

**LENNOX, MARGARET**, relict of Alexander Bell a merchant bailie of Dundee, testament, 1724, 1725, CB. [NAS]

**LIDDELL, Mrs ELIZABETH**, vintner in Dundee, 1748, testament, 1776, CB. [NAS.E326.1.50]

**LINDSAY, HELEN**, in Dundee, testament, 1787, CB. [NAS]

**LINDSAY, ROBERT**, workman in Dundee, testament, 1742, CB.

**LIVINGSTONE, DAVID**, writer in Dundee, 1799. [DCA.B19.3.27/253]

**LOGAN, WILLIAM**, skipper in Dundee, testament, 1785, CB.

**LOW, ALEXANDER**, merchant in Dundee & part-owner of the James of Dundee, 1716, 1728. [NAS.AC9.565/1062]

**LOW, JAMES**, merchant in Dundee, spouse Elizabeth Mitchell, 1743; testament, 1754, CB. [NAS.RH11.70.7]

**LOW, ROBERT**, merchant in Dundee, 1791. [DCA.B19.3.27/262]

**LOW, WILLIAM**, b.1750, d.1812, wife Janet Glenday, b.1756, d.1802. [HMI]

**LOWDEN, DAVID**, b. 1739, d. 1811. [HMI]

**LOWDEN, GILBERT**, carter in Hilltown, Dundee, 1792. [DCA.B19.3.27/1/12]

**LOWDEN, SAMUEL**, Customs surveyor in Dundee, testament, 1747, 1749, CB. [NAS]

**LOWNIE, WILLIAM**, b. 1673, a tailor in Dundee, d. 1740, wife Sarah Young, b. 1663, d. 1738. [HMI]

**LOWSON, THOMAS**, b.1724, resident of Dundee, d.1798, wife Margaret Bailie, b.1732, d.1782. [HMI]

**LUGGATT, JOHN**, slater in Dundee, testament, 1709, CB.

**LUMSDEN, DAVID**, merchant in Dundee, 1737. [NAS.AC9.1384]

# THE PEOPLE OF DUNDEE, 1700-1799

**LUMSDEN, WALTER,** merchant in Dundee, testament, 1779, CB. [NAS]
**LUNDIE, JAMES,** bookseller in Dundee, testament, 1769, CB.
**LUNDIE, JOHN,** merchant in Dundee, testament, 1730, CB.
**LUNDIE, THOMAS,** merchant & bailie of Dundee, 1737, 1748. [NAS.AC9.1384; E326.1.50]
**LYON, AGNES,** spouse to Thomas Black a surgeon in Dundee, testament, 1748, CB. [NAS]
**LYON, CHARLES,** apprentice silversmith in Dundee, 1745. [JA]
**LYON, DAVID,** merchant in Dundee, 1711. [NAS.AC9.378]
**LYON, GEORGE,** merchant & bailie of Dundee, husband of Janet Duncan, sasine, 1747, testament, 1748, CB. [NAS.RS35.16.579]
**LYON, GEORGE,** jr., testament, 1753, CB. [NAS]
**LYON, ISOBEL,** relict of William Forrest wright in Dundee, testament, 1746, CB. [NAS]
**LYON, JAMES,** inn-keeper in Dundee, 1745, 1748. [JA][NAS.E326.1.50]
**LYON, JOHN,** of Kinnaird, merchant in Dundee, 1765, father of David Lyon a merchant in London, 1799. [DCA.B19.3.27/239]
**LYON, PATRICK,** baker in Dundee, 1748. [NAS.E326.1.50]
**LYON, WILLIAM,** merchant in Dundee, 1715. [NAS.AC9.540]
**LYON, Madam,** in Dundee, 1748. [NAS.E326.1.50]
**MCARTHUR, DAVID,** gardener in Dundee, testament, 1758, CB. [NAS]
**MCCOMIE, THOMAS,** b.1750, weaver in Hawkhill, d.1790. [HMI]
**MCCOWAN, JOHN,** from Dundee, a member of the Scots Charitable Society of Boston, 1758. [SCS/NEHGS]
**MCCROCKAT, GEORGE,** coppersmith in Dundee, testament, 1777, 1783, CB. [NAS]
**MACDONALD, JOHN,** servant in Dundee, 1745. [JA]
**MCEWAN, JAMES,** weaver in Dundee, 1748. [NAS.E326.1.50]
**MCEWEN, JAMES,** b. 1750, minister of the Associated Anti-Burgher Congregation of Dundee, d. 1813. [HMI]
**MCEWAN, WILLIAM,** minister in Dundee, testament, 1762, CB. [NAS]
**MCGREGOR or GRANT, DONALD,** pensioner in Dundee, testament, 1780, CB. [NAS]

# THE PEOPLE OF DUNDEE, 1700-1799

**MCINTOSH, ISOBEL,** servant in Dundee, testament, 1796, CB.
**MACINTOSH, WILLIAM,** servant in Dundee, 1745. [JA]
**MACKAY, JAMES,** merchant in Dundee, 1770s. [HMI]
**MCKAY, NEIL,** in Dundee, 1748. [NAS.E326.1.50]
**MACKAY, PATRICK,** merchant in Dundee, testament, 1786, CB. [NAS]
**MCLAGAN, JOHN,** in Logerait then at the West Port of Dundee, sasine, 1779. [NAS.RS35.27.414]
**MCLEAN, DUNCAN,** b. 1749, a merchant in Petersburg, Virginia, d. there on 10 April 1814. [Howff gravestone]
**MACHAN, MARGARET,** relict of Robert Philp skipper in Dundee, testament, 1758, CB. [NAS]
**MACHAN, ROBERT,** mariner in Dundee, 1716. [NAS.AC9.563]
**MAIDEN, WILLIAM,** shoemaker in Dundee, testament, 1770, 1773, CB. [NAS]
**MAIDEN, WILLIAM,** merchant in Dundee, testament, 1796, CB. [NAS]
**MALTMAN, WILLIAM,** burgess of Dundee, testament, 1710, CB. [NAS]
**MANN, JAMES,** merchant & bailie of Dundee, sasine, 1704, testament, 1713, 1720, CB. [NAS.RS35.10.577]
**MANN, JOHN,** merchant in Dundee, testament, 1738, CB.
**MANN, ROBERT,** merchant in Dundee, testament, 1749, CB.
**MARDER, JOHN,** Deacon of the Dyers in Dundee, 1748. [NAS.E326.1.50]
**MARR, JOHN,** jr., master of the Helen of Dundee, 1706. [NAS.AC9.238]
**MARR, PATRICK,** b.1740, brewer in Dundee,d.1770, spouse Isobel Richard, testament, 1777, CB. [NAS]
**MARSHALL, DAVID,** skipper in Dundee, testament, 1760, CB.
**MARSHALL, JAMES,** Convenor in Dundee, 1748. [NAS.E326.1.50]
**MARSHALL, PATRICK,** merchant from Dundee, settled in South Carolina, later in New Providence, probate 1760, the Bahamas.
**MARSHALL, WILLIAM,** merchant in Dundee, d. 1781, testament, 1781, CB, wife Christian Pilmore b. 1720, d. 1751. [HMI]

# THE PEOPLE OF DUNDEE, 1700-1799

**MARSHALL, WILLIAM,** merchant in Dundee, 1748, 1799. [NAS.E326.1.50; DCA.B19.3.27/159]

**MARTIN, DAVID,** brewer in Dundee, 1748. [NAS.E326.1.50]

**MARTIN, JAMES,** emigrated to Charleston, South Carolina, in 1771, baker & merchant in Savannah, Georgia, a Loyalist who returned to Dundee after 1776. [NA.AO13.36.697-705]

**MARTIN, JAMES,** wife Isabel Stratton, b.1759, d.1790. [HMI]

**MARTIN, JAMES,** bookseller in Dundee, 1799. [DCA.B19.3.27/266]

**MARTIN, JOHN,** brewer in Dundee, 1748. [NAS.E326.1.50]

**MARTIN, PATRICK,** in Hawkhill, wife Janet Bower, b.1751, d.1811. [HMI]

**MATHERS, JOHN,** flesher in Dundee, 1725, wife Rachel Brisbane, b.1701, d.1740. [NAS.AC9.943][HMI]

**MATHERS, SAMUEL,** b.1735, flesher in Dundee, d.1812, wife Christian Murdoch, b.1733, d.1816. [HMI]

**MATTHEW, GEORGE,** dyer in Dundee, 1748. [NAS.E326.1.50]

**MATTHEW, GEORGE,** b. 1740, maltman in Dundee, d. 1801, wife Janet Wood, b. 1748, d. 1796. [HMI]

**MATTHEW, JAMES,** brewer in Dundee, 1748. [NAS.E326.1.50]

**MATTHEW, JAMES,** weaver in Dundee, books, 1787-1789. [NAS.CS96.3188-3189]

**MATTHEW, JAMES,** jr., manufacturer in Dundee, 1799, son of James Matthew sr. & his wife Isobel, daughter of James Flowers a manufacturer in Dundee. [DCA.B19.3.27/215]

**MATTHEW, THOMAS,** clerk of the Dundee Ropeworks, 1746. [NAS.AC8.671]

**MATTHEW, THOMAS,** brewer in Dundee, 1748. [NAS.E326.1.50]

**MATHEWSON, ROBERT,** born 1729, manufacturer in Dundee, d.1802. [HMI]

**MAWER, GEORGE,** dyer in Dundee, 1748. [NAS.E326.1.50]

**MAWER, ROBERT,** skipper in Dundee, testament, 1737, CB.

**MAWER, ROBERT,** dyer in Dundee, 1748, testament, 1771, CB. [NAS.E326.1.50]

**MAXWELL, ALEXANDER,** merchant in Dundee, 1714. [NAS.AC11.12]

# THE PEOPLE OF DUNDEE, 1700-1799

**MAXWELL, DAVID,** merchant in Dundee, bailie there, provost, 1714, 1715, 1718, 1725, 1746, 1748. [NAS.AC11.12; AC9.540/910; B59.30.46; NRAS.150.3.22; E326.1.50]
**MAXWELL, DAVID,** of Bogmiln, merchant in Dundee, 1757. [NRAS.150.3.24/25/27]
**MAXWELL, GEORGE,** merchant in Dundee, 1748. [NAS.E326.1.50]
**MAXWELL, GEORGE,** of Balmyle, provost of Dundee, testament, 1796, CB. [NAS]
**MAXWELL, JAMES,** brewer in Dundee, 1748, testament, 1751, CB. [NAS.E326.1.50]
**MAXWELL, JOHN,** mariner in Dundee, testament, 1717, CB.
**MAXWELL, PATRICK,** merchant & provost of Dundee, d. 1737, ? testament, 1766, CB; father of William, Patrick, & David, 1749. [HMI] [NAS.AC8.718]
**MAXWELL, PATRICK,** Customs controller in Dundee, testament,1797, CB. [NAS]
**MAXWELL, WILLIAM,** merchant & baillie of Dundee, testament, 1786, CB. [NAS]
**MAXWELL, Madam,** in Dundee, 1748. [NAS.E326.1.50]
**MEALL, ROBERT,** b. 1687, tailor in Dundee, d. 1744. [HMI]
**MELDRUM, ALEXANDER,** ships carpenter in Dundee, 1788. [NAS.SC20.36.15]
**MENZIES, WILLIAM,** sailor in Dundee, testament, 1746, CB.
**METHVEN, JAMES,** painter in Dundee, testament, 1786, CB.
**MILLER, ANDREW,** in Dundee, 1748. [NAS.E326.1.50]
**MILLER, CHARLES,** b. 1732, manufacturer, d. 1812, wife Christian Blair, b. 1736, d. 1800. [HMI]
**MILLAR, DAVID,** master of the Neptune of Dundee, 1726. [NAS.AC8.337]
**MILLER, JAMES,** horse-hirer in Dundee, 1745. [JA]
**MILLER, JAMES,** b. 1715, d. 1789. [HMI]
**MILLAR, JAMES,** skipper in Dundee, testament, 1759, CB.
**MILLAR, JOHN,** brewer in West Ferry, testament, 1758, CB.
**MILLAR, JOHN,** merchant in Dundee, testament, 1769, CB.
**MILLER, JOHN,** b. 1764, d. 1788, son of Patrick Miller a tailor in Dundee & his wife Jean Brown. [HMI]
**MILLAR, PATRICK,** maltman in Dundee, testament, 1770, CB.
**MILLAR, THOMAS,** merchant in Dundee, testament, 1785, CB.
**MILLAR, THOMAS,** skipper in Dundee, d,1809. [HMI]

# THE PEOPLE OF DUNDEE, 1700-1799

**MILLAR, WILLIAM,** Customs controller at Dundee, 1714. [NAS.AC9.509]

**MILLER, WILLIAM,** sailor in Dundee, 1745. [JA]

**MILLER, WILLIAM,** in Dundee, 1748. [NAS.E326.1.50]; possibly a merchant, testament, 1770, CB. [NAS]

**MILLAR, WILLIAM,** skipper in Dundee, testament, 1763, CB.

**MILLS, ELIZABETH,** from Dundee, emigrated via Kirkcaldy to Brunswick, North Carolina, aboard the Jamaica Packet of Burntisland in June 1775. [NA.T47.12]

**MILLS, JOHN,** joiner from Dundee, emigrated via Kirkcaldy to Brunswick, North Carolina, aboard the Jamaica Packet of Burntisland in June 1775. [NA.T47.12]

**MILNE, ALEXANDER,** weaver in Dundee, testament, 1769, 1775, CB. [NAS]

**MILNE, DAVID,** brewer in Dundee, testament, 1787, CB. [NAS]

**MILNE, JAMES,** merchant in Dundee, 1748. [NAS.E326.1.50]

**MILN, JAMES,** wright in Dundee, 1796. [DCA.B19.3.26/1]

**MILNE, JOHN,** merchant in Dundee, 1748. [NAS.E326.1.50]

**MILNE, ROBERT,** dyer in Dundee, 1748. [NAS.E326.1.50]; ? dyer & candlemaker in Dundee, testament, 1776, CB.

**MILN, WILLIAM,** merchant in Dundee, 1737, 1748, testament, 1769, CB. [NAS.AC9.1384; E326.1.50]

**MITCHELL, ANN,** in Dundee, testament, 1793, CB. [NAS]

**MITCHELL, CHARLES,** writer in Dundee, testament, 1777, CB. [NAS]

**MITCHELL, DAVID,** brewer in Dundee, 1748. [NAS.E326.1.50]

**MITCHELL, JAMES,** maltman in Dundee, husband of Margaret Webster, b. 1716, d. 1745. [HMI]

**MITCHELL, JAMES,** ropemaker in Dundee, 1778. [NAS.RS35.27.6]

**MITCHELL, JAMES,** clerk to John Ogilvie a writer in Dundee, 1792. [NRAS.124.4.2.59]

**MITCHELL, JOHN,** merchant in Dundee, 1725. [NAS.AC9.910]

**MITCHELL, JOHN,** wright in Dundee, testament, 1766, CB.

**MITCHELL, PATRICK,** merchant in Dundee, 1798.. [DCA.B19.3.27/15]

**MITCHELL, WILLIAM,** minister in Dundee, testament, 1713, 1714, CB; widow Margaret Cant, 1722. [NAS.AC9.792]

# THE PEOPLE OF DUNDEE, 1700-1799

**MITCHELL, WILLIAM,** maltman in Dundee, testament, 1736, CB. [NAS]

**MITCHELL, WILLIAM,** b. 1702, merchant in Glasgow later in Dundee, d. 1770, wife Margaret Orme, b. 1705, d. 1767. [HMI][NAS.E326.1.50]

**MITCHELL, WILLIAM,** merchant trading between Dundee & Carolina, 1772. [NAS.E504.11.8]

**MITCHELL, WILLIAM,** ship carpenter in Dundee, sasine, 1757. [NAS.RS35.18.376]

**MITCHELL, Dr WILLIAM,** b. 1742, physician in Dundee, d. 1784, wife Agnes Carnegy, b. 1744, d. 1825. [HMI]

**MITCHELSON, ANDREW,** merchant in Dundee, testament, 1737, CB. [NAS]

**MITCHELSON, JOHN,** weaver in Hilltown, sasine, 1767. [NAS.RS35.22.18]

**MONRO, JOHN,** shoemaker in Dundee, husb& of Margaret Wright, b. 1734, d. 1771. [HMI]

**MONRO, THOMAS,** in Overgate, Dundee, 1798.. [DCA.B19.3.27/11]

**MONTEITH, ROBERT,** maltman & brewer in Dundee, wife Isabel Smith, b.1683, d.1732. [HMI]

**MOODIE, GEORGE,** bailie of Dundee, 1748. [NAS.E326.1.50]

**MOODIE, JOHN,** weaver in Dundee, 1748. [NAS.E326.1.50]

**MOODIE, PATRICK,** weaver in Dundee, 1748. [NAS.E326.1.50]

**MOODIE, ROBERT,** weaver in Dundee, 1748. [NAS.E326.1.50]

**MOODIE, THOMAS,** bailie of Dundee, testament, 1707, CB.

**MOODIE, THOMAS,** weaver in Dundee, 1748. [NAS.E326.1.50]

**MOODIE, WILLIAM,** brewer in Dundee, 1748. [NAS.E326.1.50]

**MOORE, WILLIAM,** horse-hirer in Dundee, 1745. [JA]

**MORRIS, JAMES,** weaver burgess of Dundee, testament, 1712, CB. [NAS]

**MORISON, ALEXANDER,** manufacturer in Dundee, 1776. [NAS.B59.25.2.84]

**MORISON, ALEXANDER,** merchant in Dundee, an account book, 1795-1797. [NAS.CS96/3840]

**MORRISON, JOHN,** in the Ferry, Dundee, 1748. [NAS.E326.1.50]

# THE PEOPLE OF DUNDEE, 1700-1799

**MORISON, JOHN,** vintner in Dundee, testament, 1755, CB.
**MORRISON, ROBERT,** merchant in Dundee, 1718. [NAS.AC9.630]
**MORISON, THOMAS,** skipper in Dundee, testament, 1731, 1733, CB. [NAS]
**MORRISON, WILLIAM,** merchant in Dundee & part-owner of the James of Dundee, 1716, 1725. [NAS.AC9.565/910]
**MORRISON, WILLIAM,** in Dundee, 1748. [NAS.E326.1.50]
**MORRISON, WILLIAM,** of Naughton, in Dundee, 1748. [NAS.E326.1.50]
**MORISON, WILLIAM,** merchant & bailie of Dundee, testament, 1753, CB. [NAS]
**MORISON, WILLIAM,** merchant in Dundee, an account book, 1795-1797. [NAS.CS96.3840]
**MORRICE, WILLIAM,** weaver in Dundee, 1748. [NAS.E326.1.50]
**MORTON, MUNGO,** manufacturer in Dundee, 1796. [DCA.B19.3.26/6]
**MUDIE, JAMES,** skipper in Dundee, testament, 1797, CB.
**MUDIE, THOMAS,** weaver in Dundee, 1745. [JA]
**MURRAY, ALEXANDER,** merchant in Dundee, 1748. [NAS.E326.1.50]
**MURRAY, JAMES,** vintner in Dundee, relict Margaret Rodger, 1741. [NAS.SC20.36.7]
**MURRAY, JOHN,** of Lintrose, bailie of Dundee, 1736, 1748. [NAS.AC10.240; E326.1.50]
**MURRISON, THOMAS,** boy on the James of Dundee, 1716. [NAS.AC9.565]
**MURRISON, WILLIAM,** seaman on the James of Dundee, 1716. [NAS.AC9.565]
**MYLES, ALEXANDER.** b.1761, skipper in Dundee, d. 1828, wife Catherine Meldrum, b.1766, died 1814. [HMI]
**MYLES, WILLIAM,** d. 1754. [HMI]
**NAIRNE, JOHN,** b. 1735, shipmaster in Dundee, d. 1812. Husb& of Anne Watson, b. 1725, d. 1760. [HMI]
**NAISMITH, JOHN,** wool-weaver in Dundee, 1745. [JA]
**NAISMITH, ROBERT,** in Dundee, 1745. [JA]
**NASH, JOHN,** servant in Dundee, 1745. [JA]
**NEAVE, THOMAS,** b.1734, d.1813. [HMI]
**NEILSON, GEORGE,** skipper in Dundee, 1764. [HMI]

# THE PEOPLE OF DUNDEE, 1700-1799

**NICHOLL, DAVID,** merchant in Dundee, a burgess ticket, 1797; a merchant at East Port, Dundee, wife Margaret Scott, b. 1743, d. 1821. [NRAS.1684/9][HMI]
**NICOLL, DAVID,** b.1737, manufacturer in Dundee, d,1807, wife Janet Begbie. [HMI]
**NICOLL, GEORGE,** late of Jamaica, then in Dundee, 1790. [DCA.B19.3.27/9]
**NICOLL, JOHN,** b. 1747, merchant in Dundee, d. 1778. [HMI]
**NICOLL, JOHN,** officer to the Dean of Guild of Dundee, 1798.. [DCA.B19.3.27/6]
**NORIE, ROBERT,** seaman on the James of Dundee, 1716. [NAS.AC9.565]
**OGILVIE, ALEXANDER,** deputy shoremaster of Dundee; 1747.. [NAS.AC11.176]
**OGILVIE, GEORGE,** maltmaker in Dundee, 1703. [NAS.AC9.32]
**OGILVY, GEORGE,** of Baikie, a merchant in Dundee, husband of Margaret Erskine, 1779, 1783. [NRAS.124.4.2]
**OGILVIE, GEORGE,** merchant in Dundee, 1799. [DCA.B19.3.27/162]
**OGILVIE, HENRY,** in Dundee, 1748. [NAS.E326.1.50]
**OGILVIE, JAMES,** merchant in Dundee, 1714. [NAS.AC11.12]
**OGILVY, JAMES,** merchant in Dundee, a witness,1783. [NRAS.124.4.2]
**OGILVIE, JEAN,** b.1723, d.1770. [HMI]
**OGILVIE, JOHN,** merchant from Dundee, in Charleston, South Carolina, 1785. [NAS.CS17.1.4/28]
**OGILVIE, JOHN,** writer in Dundee, 1792, 1799. [NRAS.124.4.2.59; DCA.B19.3.27/202]
**OGILVIE, THOMAS,** maltman in Dundee, 1706. [NAS.AC8.65]
**OGILVIE, THOMAS,** merchant in Dundee, 1745. [JA]
**OGILVIE, THOMAS,** of Cowle, in Dundee, 1748. [NAS.E326.1.50]
**OGILVIE, WILLIAM,** rector of Dundee Grammar School, d. 1727. [HMI]
**OLIPHANT, JOHN,** merchant in Dundee, 1705, 1714, husband of Elizabeth Craig; bailie & dean of guild of Dundee, 1711, 1715; former owner of the George of Dundee, 1718. [NAS.AC9.540; AC13.1.30; AC13.1.212; B59.24.15.6; RD4.88.777] [JA]

# THE PEOPLE OF DUNDEE, 1700-1799

**OLIPHANT, WILLIAM,** merchant in Dundee, 1714. [NAS.RD4.89.66]

**ORAM, Mrs,** in Dundee, 1748. [NAS.E326.1.50]

**ORME, HENRY,** b. 1655, merchant in Dundee, d. 1732, wife Margaret Stratton, b. 1667, d. 1734. [HMI]

**ORROCK, JOHN,** Customs officer in Dundee, 1745, 1748. [NAS.E326.1.50][JA]

**OUCHTERLONY, JOHN,** mason in Dundee, 1745. [JA]

**OUCHTERLONY, PETER,** coffee house keeper in Dundee, 1745. [JA]

**PAGE, THOMAS,** weaver in Dundee, 1748. [NAS.E326.1.50]

**PATERSON, DAVID,** merchant in Dundee, 1746. [NAS.AC8.675]

**PATERSON, GEORGE,** master of the James of Dundee, 1704, 1716. [NAS.AC9.66/565; AC8.198]

**PATERSON, JAMES,** merchant in Dundee, 1715, part-owner of the James of Dundee, 1716. [NAS.AC9.540/565]

**PATERSON, JAMES,** workman in Dundee, 1745. [JA]

**PATERSON, JAMES,** merchant in Overgate, Dundee, 1798. [DCA.B19.3.27/11]

**PATERSON, Mrs,** in Dundee, 1748. [NAS.E326.1.50]

**PATON, HENDRY,** b.1694, maltman in Dundee, d.1742. [HMI]

**PATTON, HENRY,** hatter in Dundee, 1799. [DCA.B19.3.27/268]

**PATTULLO, GEORGE,** merchant in Dundee, 1745. [JA]

**PATTULLO, HENRY,** merchant in Dundee, 1745; dead by 1748. [JA][NAS.E326.1.50]

**PEARSON, JAMES,** baker in Dundee, 1722. [NAS.AC9.792]

**PECK, JOSEPH,** in Dundee, 1748. [NAS.E326.1.50]

**PEDDIE, ANDREW,** b. 1744, merchant in Dundee, d.1810, wife Elizabeth How, b. 1750, d.1819. [HMI]

**PETER, JOHN,** b.1738, builder in Dundee, 1798, 1799, d.1813, wife Mary Hog, b.1734, d.1794. [NAS.SC20.33.1][HMI] [DCA.B19.3.27/266]

**PETRIE, ANDREW,** workman in Dundee, 1745. [JA]

**PETRIE, GEORGE,** master of the Samuel of Dundee, 1744. [NAS.AC11.159]

**PHILIPS, ALEXANDER,** boat-builder in Dundee, wife Catherine Crombie, b.1762, d.1792. [HMI]

# THE PEOPLE OF DUNDEE, 1700-1799

**PHILLIPS, Major WILLIAM,** b. 1744, d. 1813, wife Catherine Nicoll, b. 1744, d. 1811. [HMI]
**PHILP, ROBERT,** skipper in Dundee, 1746. [NAS.AC8.670]
**PHILP, THOMAS,** skipper in North Ferry of Dundee, 1746. [NAS.AC8.671]
**PIRIE, GILBERT,** weaver in Hilltown, wife May Mudie, b.1752, d.1812. [HMI]
**PITCAIRN, ANDREW,** writer in Dundee, 1798. [DCA.B19.3.27/11]
**PITCAIRN, JOHN,** merchant in Dundee, 1766, d. 1800. [NAS.CS16.1.125/247][HMI]
**PITCAIRN, ROBERT,** b. 1694, writer in Dundee, 1748, d. 1753, wife Jean Jobson. [HMI][NAS.E326.1.50]
**PLAYFAIR, JAMES,** maltman in Dundee, wife Janet Patterson, b.1757, d.1784. [HMI]
**PLAYFAIR, THOMAS,** b.1742, brewer in Seagate, d.1809. [HMI]
**PLAYFAIR, WILLIAM,** b. 1718, d. 1735. [HMI]
**PRESTON, ALEXANDER,** merchant in Dundee, 1714, 1717. [NAS.RD2.85.294; AC9.607]
**PROCTOR, ANDREW,** glover in Dundee, 1748. [NAS.E326.1.50]
**PROCTOR, DAVID,** b. 1746, baker in Dundee, d. 1782. [HMI]
**PROCTOR, JOHN,** b. 1721, baker in Dundee, d. 1776, his spouse Isobel Crichton, b. 1729, d. 1804. [HMI]
**PROCTOR, ROBERT,** in Dundee, 1735. [NAS.B59.38.2.164]
**PROFFITT, Mrs,** in Dundee, 1748. [NAS.E326.1.50]
**RAIT, JAMES,** merchant in Overgate, Dundee, 1747, 1748, relict Isobel Ramsay, 1798. [NAS.B59.38.6.132; E326.1.50; DCA.B19.3.27/9]
**RAIT, JOHN,** skipper in Dundee, 1704. [NAS.AC9.70]
**RAIT, Dr JOHN,** in Dundee, 1748. [NAS.E326.1.50]
**RAIT, ROBERT,** master of the Alexander of Dundee, 1710; master of the George of Dundee, 1711. [NAS.AC9.369; AC8.138]
**RAIT, WILLIAM,** surgeon in Dundee, 1745. [JA]
**RAMSAY, DAVID,** sr., merchant in Dundee, 1710, 1718, 1737. [NAS.AC9.359/1384; AC13.1.212]
**RAMSAY, DAVID,** skipper in Dundee, 1710; master of the David of Dundee, 1721. [NAS.AC9.359; AC8.265][HMI]

# THE PEOPLE OF DUNDEE, 1700-1799

**RAMSAY, DAVID,** baxter in Dundee, 1714. [NAS.RD4.89.623]
**RAMSAY, DAVID,** brewer in Dundee, 1748. [NAS.E326.1.50]
**RAMSAY, GEORGE,** merchant in Dundee, 1714. [NAS.AC11.12]
**RAMSAY, GEORGE,** jr., merchant in Dundee, 1729. [NAS.AC8.394]
**RAMSAY, GEORGE,** weaver in Dundee, 1745. [JA]
**RAMSAY, JAMES,** b.1690, merchant in Dundee, d.1753. [NAS.E326.1.50][HMI]
**RAMSAY, JOHN,** merchant & bailie of Dundee, 1715, 1745, 1748. [NAS.AC9.540; E326.1.50][JA]
**RAMSAY, ROBERT,** brewer in Dundee, 1748. [NAS.E326.1.50]
**RAMSAY, Mrs,** in Dundee, 1748. [NAS.E326.1.50]
**RAMSAY, Miss,** in Dundee, 1748. [NAS.E326.1.50]
**RANKIN, ALEXANDER,** merchant in Dundee, 1714. [NAS.AC11.12]
**RANKIN, ALEXANDER,** mariner in Dundee, 1714. [NAS.AC11.12]
**RANKINE, JOHN,** merchant trading between Dundee & South Carolina, 1770s. [NAS.E504.11]
**RANKINE, WILLIAM,** merchant in Dundee, 1748. [NAS.E326.1.50]
**RATTRAY, DAVID,** b.1760, manufacturer in Dens, d.1811, wife Mary Scott. [HMI]
**RATTRAY, GEORGE,** brewer in Dundee, 1748. [NAS.E326.1.50]
**RATTRAY, JAMES,** ropemaker in Dundee, 1745. [JA]
**RATTRAY, JAMES,** brewer in Dundee, 1748. [NAS.E326.1.50]
**REID, ALEXANDER,** jr., merchant in Dundee, 1705, 1710. [NAS.AC9.120; AC9.359]
**REID, Captain ALEXANDER,** in Logie, Dundee, 1748. [NAS.E326.1.50]
**REID, DAVID,** wife Elizabeth Dempster b.1753, d. 1780. [HMI]
**REID, THOMAS,** skipper of Dundee, 1704. [NAS.AC8.23]
**REID, THOMAS,** merchant in Dundee, 1706. [NAS.AC8.65]
**REID, THOMAS,** merchant in Dundee, 1748. [NAS.E326.1.50]
**REID, THOMAS,** son of Thomas Reid a merchant in Dundee, a merchant in Jamaica, 1766. [NAS.RS35.16.21.439]
**RENNEY, JOHN,** b. 1711, merchant in Dundee, d. 1756. [HMI]

# THE PEOPLE OF DUNDEE, 1700-1799

**RICHARDSON, JAMES,** bonnetmaker in Hilltown, sasine, 1704. [NAS.RS35.1.335]
**RIDDOCH, ALEXANDER,** b. 1744, d. 1822, provost of Dundee & deputy lieutenant of Forfarshire. [HMI]
**RIOCH, PATRICK,** master of the Neptune of Dundee, 1722. [NAS.AC9.792]
**ROBB, JOHN,** weaver in Dundee, 1748. [NAS.E326.1.50]
**ROBERTSON, ALEXANDER,** merchant in Dundee, 1714. [NAS.AC11.12; RD4.88.771]
**ROBERTSON, ALEXANDER,** merchant in Dundee, 1737, 1745. [NAS.AC9.1384][JA][NAS.E326.1.50]
**ROBERTSON, ALEXANDER,** b. 1694, merchant & provost of Dundee, d. 1775, wife Ann Scrymsoure, b. 1702, d. 1775. [HMI][NAS.E326.1.50]
**ROBERTSON, DAVID,** boat-builder in Dundee, 1784, 1796. [NAS.SC20.36.14; B59.24.1.86]
**ROBERTSON, DUNCAN,** in Dundee, 1748. [NAS.E326.1.50]
**ROBERTSON, JAMES,** b. 1726, thread maker in Dundee, d. 1798. [HMI]
**ROBERTSON, JAMES,** b.1751, sailor. D.1778, wife Christian Ambrose, b.1744, d.1803. [HMI]
**ROBERTSON, JOHN,** merchant in Dundee, 1714. [NAS.AC11.12]
**ROBERTSON, JOHN,** founder in Dundee, 1748. [NAS.E326.1.50]
**ROBERTSON, PETER,** apprentice in Dundee, 1745. [JA]
**ROBERTSON, ROBERT,** b.1721, musician, d.1808, wife (1) Chirsten Drummond, b.1736, d.1776, (2) Agnes Coupar, b.1745, d.1815. [HMI]
**ROBERTSON, THOMAS,** in Dundee, 1748. [NAS.E326.1.50]
**ROBERTSON, THOMAS,** from Dundee, a member of the Scots Charitable Society of Boston, 1753. [SCS/NEHGS]
**ROBERTSON, THOMAS,** merchant trading between Dundee & Virginia, 1771. [NAS.E504.11.7]
**RODGER, WILLIAM,** merchant in Dundee, relict Euphan Mann, 1740. [NAS.CS16.1.69]
**ROGER, CHARLES,** b.1731, manufacturer in Dundee, d.1799, wife Katherine Young. [HMI]
**ROLLO, ANDREW,** skipper in Dundee, 1718. [NAS.AC9.630]

# THE PEOPLE OF DUNDEE, 1700-1799

**ROLLO, ROBERT,** skipper in Dundee, & spouse Ann Whittet, 1726. [DCA.B19.3.27/4, 7]

**ROSS, CHARLES,** b.1750, merchant in Dundee, d.1826, wife (1) Elisabeth Clark, b.1764, d.1809, (2) Jean Mitchell, b.1772, d.1846. [HMI]

**ROSS, DAVID,** master of the Mayflower of Dundee, 1725. [NAS.AC9.910]

**ROSS, ROBERT,** skipper in Dundee, master of the Buckstone, 1748. [NAS.AC8.725; E326.1.50]

**SALTER, DAVID,** brewer in Dundee, 1748. [NAS.E326.1.50]

**SALTER, WILLIAM,** victualler & maltman in Dundee, 1745. [JA]

**SANDEMAN, DAVID,** merchant in Dundee, 1737, 1746, 1748, 1750; wife Euphemia Lyon, b.1721, d.1742. [HMI] [NAS.AC8.670; AC9.1384; AC11.189; E326.1.50]

**SANDEMAN, WILLIAM,** merchant in Dundee, & bleacher at Douglas Bleachfield, 1799. [DCA.B19.3.27/185/190]

**SCOTT, ALEXANDER,** weaver in Blackscroft, wife Isobel Tyrie, b.1749, d.1810. [HMI]

**SCOTT, JAMES,** b. 1751, mason in Hawkhill, d. 1807, wife Janet Bell, b. 1764, d. 1800. [HMI]

**SCOTT, JAMES,** b.1746, merchant in Dundee, d.1823, wife Elisabeth Stewart, b.1744, d.1808. [HMI]

**SCOTT, JOHN,** merchant in Dundee, 1710, 1711. [NAS.AC9.359/403]

**SCOTT, JOHN,** brewer in Dundee, 1748. [NAS.E326.1.50]

**SCOTT, PATRICK,** skipper & baillie of Dundee, testament, 1737, CB. [NAS]

**SCOTT, ROBERT,** wright in Dundee, testament, 1776, CB.

**SCOTT, THOMAS,** merchant & former bailie of Dundee, 1717/1718. [NAS.AC13.1.212; AC9.607]

**SCOTT, WALTER,** Customs surveyor at Dundee, 1723; testament, 1723, CB . [NAS.AC9.813]

**SCOTT, WILLIAM,** merchant in Dundee, 1748, testament, 1757, CB. [NAS.E326.1.50]

**SCOTT, WILLIAM,** jeweller in Dundee, testament, 1800, CB.

**SCRYMGEOUR, ALEXANDER,** of Fellan, in Dundee, 1748. [NAS.E326.1.50]

**SCRYMGEOUR, JOHN,** of Tealing, merchant & provost of Dundee, testament, 1735, CB. [NAS]

# THE PEOPLE OF DUNDEE, 1700-1799

**SHAW, JAMES,** servant in Dundee, 1745. [JA]
**SHEPHERD, LAUCHLAND,** writer in Dundee, testament, 1718, CB. [NAS]
**SHEPHERD, MUNGO,** merchant in Dundee, 1798. [DCA.B19.3.27/13]
**SIMM, DAVID,** merchant in Dundee, 1766. [NAS.CS16.1.125/247]
**SIMPSON, ANDREW,** sailor in Dundee, 1745. [JA]
**SIMPSON, ARTHUR,** skipper of Dundee, 1732, 1735. [NAS.AC8.445; AC10.212]
**SIVEWRIGHT, ROBERT,** b. 1743, shipmaster in Dundee, d. 1807, spouse Christian Thain, b. 1755, d. 1788. [HMI]
**SKIRLING, PATRICK,** brewer or maltman in Dundee, 1748, testament, 1756, CB; wife Elizabeth, b.1696, d.1732. [NAS.E326.1.50][HMI]
**SKIRLING, ROBERT,** brewer in Dundee, 1748. [NAS.E326.1.50]
**SKIRLING, THOMAS,** gardener in Dundee, testament, 1758, CB. [NAS]
**SKIRLING, WILLIAM,** maltman in Dundee, d.1718. [HMI]
**SKIRLING, WILLIAM,** in Dundee, 1748. [NAS.E326.1.50]
**SLATER, DAVID,** maltman in Dundee, 1752. [NAS.RD3.211.288]
**SMALL, ANDREW,** in Dundee, testament, 1735, CB. [NAS]
**SMALL, ANDREW,** b.1753, weaver in Hawkhill, d. 1816, husband of Isabel Nicol. [HMI]
**SMALL, JOHN,** in Dundee, 1745. [JA]
**SMALL, WILLIAM,** writer in Dundee, 1798; wife Jean Davidson, b.1717, d.1782. [DCA.B19.3.27/8][HMI]
**SMART, ANDREW,** b.1676, mason and architect in Dundee, d.1736, wife Anne Shephers, b.1695, d.1758. [HMI]
**SMART, DAVID,** b. 1731, baker in Dundee, d. 1806. [HMI]
**SMART, JAMES,** b.1699, mason in Dundee, d.1756, wife Janet Donaldson, b.1701, d.1753. [HMI]
**SMART, JAMES,** b. 1747, baker in Dundee, d. 1798, spouse Ann Norval, b. 1759, d. 1834. [HMI]
**SMART, THOMAS,** b.1726, mason, architect, burgess, & guldsbrother of Dundee, d. 1801, wife Mary Ogilvie, b.1719, d.1799. [HMI]

# THE PEOPLE OF DUNDEE, 1700-1799

**SMEATON, Captain ANDREW,** of Greenlawhill, merchant in Dundee, testament, 1723, CB. [NAS]
**SMEATON, JAMES,** merchant in Dundee, 1714. [NAS.RD2.85.379]
**SMITH, AGNES,** b.1682, schoolmistress in Dundee, d.1746. [HMI]
**SMITH, ALEXANDER,** b. 1729, d. 1802, wife Helen Baillie, b. 1733, d. 1802. [HMI]
**SMITH, GEORGE,** b.1740, tailor in Dundee, d. 1804, husband of Catherine Thomson. [HMI]
**SMITH, GILBERT,** merchant in Dundee, 1706. [NAS.AC9.239]
**SMITH, GILBERT,** brewer in Dundee, 1748. [NAS.E326.1.50]
**SMITH, HENRY,** merchant in Dundee, spouse Janet Duncan, 1703, 1714, 1721. [NAS.AC9.34/749; RD3.97.164]
**SMITH, JAMES,** skipper of North Ferry of Dundee, 1744. [NAS.AC8.649]
**SMITH, JAMES,** Convenor in Dundee, 1748. [NAS.E326.1.50]
**SMITH, JAMES,** b.1724, gardener in Chapelshade, d. 1813, wife Janet Slater, b. 1752, d. 1804. [HMI]
**SMITH, JOHN,** weaver in Hilltown, testament, 1777, CB. [NAS]
**SMITH, PATRICK,** bailie of Dundee, 1798. [DCA.B19.3.27/1]
**SMITH, ROBERT,** of Gibbstoun, in Dundee, 1748. [NAS.E326.1.50]
**SMITH, THOMAS,** butcher in Dundee, testament, 1771, CB.
**SMITH, WILLIAM,** in Dundee, 1748. [NAS.E326.1.50]
**SMITH, WILLIAM,** weaver in Dundee, 1748. [NAS.E326.1.50]
**SMYTON, JAMES,** merchant in Dundee, 1717. [NAS.AC9.607]
**SOUTAR, JAMES,** manufacturer in Dundee, 1796. [DCA.B19.3.26/1]
**SOUTAR, WILLIAM,** weaver in Dundee, 1745. [JA]
**SPANKIE, GEORGE,** weaver in Blackscroft, testament, 1784, CB. [NAS]
**SPEID, ROBERT,** writer in Dundee, 1710, 1748, testament, 1756, CB. [NAS.AC9.359; E356.1.50]]
**SPEID, THOMAS,** shoemaker in Dundee, 1748, testament, 1792, CB. [NAS.E326.1.50]
**SPEID, THOMAS,** merchant trading between Dundee & Carolina, 1771. [NAS.E504.11.7]
**SPEID, WILLIAM,** writer in Dundee, 1748. [NAS.E326.1.50]

# THE PEOPLE OF DUNDEE, 1700-1799

**SPENCE, GEORGE,** maltman in Dundee, father of George Spence in Albany Fort, North America, 1741. [NAS.RS35.16.117]
**SPENCE, GEORGE,** surgeon in Dundee, testament, 1764, 1766, CB. [NAS]
**SPENCE, JAMES,** wright in Dundee, 1706. [NAS.AC8.65]
**SPENCE, WILLIAM,** merchant in Dundee, testament, 1799, CB.
**SPINK, ANDREW,** in Dundee, dead by 1748. [NAS.E326.1.50]
**STEEL, ALEXANDER,** b.1705, dyer in Dundee, d.1773. [HMI]
**STEEL, WILLIAM,** b. 1665, dyer in Dundee, d. 1733, wife Catherine Gloik, b. 1670, d. 1745. [HMI]
**STEPHEN, WILLIAM,** merchant in Dundee, spouse Margaret Gairden, testament, 1724, CB. [NAS]
**STEPHEN, WILLIAM,** b.1734, wright in Dundee, d.1820, wife Alison Mitchell, b.1743, d.1801. [HMI]
**STEPHENS, MARGARET,** b. 1728, d. 1816. [HMI]
**STEVEN, JAMES,** Customs controller of Dundee, 1715. [NAS.AC9.540]
**STEVEN, JOHN,** b.1724, jeweller in Dundee, d.1775, wife Susanna Leslie, b. 1726, d. 1756. [HMI]
**STEVEN, WILLIAM,** merchant in Dundee, 1706, 1715. [NAS.AC9.227/540]
**STEVENSON, ALEXANDER,** b.1737, wright in Dundee, d.1781, wife Anne Talbert. [HMI]
**STEVENSON, WILLIAM,** bellman in Dundee, 1706. [NAS.AC9.216]
**STEWART, ALEXANDER,** skipper in Dundee, testament, 1745, 1750, 1752, 1771, CB. [NAS]
**STEWART, ALEXANDER,** in Dundee, 1748. [NAS.E326.1.50]
**STEWART, ANDREW,** merchant of Dundee, 1733. [NAS.AC8.473]
**STEWART, DAVID,** porter, wife (1) Barbara Allan, b.1754, d.1809, (2) Alison Farquhar. [HMI]
**STEWART, Sir GEORGE,** of Grantully, in Dundee, 1748. [NAS.E326.1.50]
**STEWART, JAMES,** Convenor of the Trades in Dundee, testament, 1721, CB. [NAS]
**STEWART, JAMES,** merchant in Dundee, 1748. [NAS.E326.1.50]
**STEWART, JAMES,** b. 1740, surgeon, d. 1821. [HMI]

THE PEOPLE OF DUNDEE, 1700-1799

**STEWART, SAMUEL,** apothecary in Dundee, 1714.
[NAS.AC9.509]
**STEWART, Madam,** in Dundee, 1748. [NAS.E326.1.50]
**STIVEN, WILLIAM,** wine-cooper in Dundee, 1745. [JA]
**STORMONTH, WILLIAM,** shipbuilder, husband of Margaret Hollems b. 1741, d. 1767. [HMI]
**STRACHAN, JAMES,** seaman on the James of Dundee, 1716. [NAS.AC9.565]
**STRACHAN, JOHN,** merchant in Dundee, 1725, 1748. [NAS.AC9.891; E326.1.50]
**STRACHAN, JOHN,** carrier in Dundee, testament, 1752, CB.
**STRACHAN, WILLIAM,** brewer in Dundee, 1748. [NAS.E326.1.50]
**STUART, ALEXANDER,** merchant in Dundee, 1745. [JA]
**STUART, JAMES,** porter in Dundee, 1745. [JA]
**STUART, JOHN,** son of James Stuart in Dundee, 1745. [JA]
**SYME, JAMES,** merchant in Dundee, books, 1746-1797. [NAS.CS96.2195/2260]
**SYME, JOHN,** surgeon in Dundee, testament, 1795, CB. [NAS]
**SYMMERS, ALEXANDER,** merchant in Dundee, testament, 1737, CB. [NAS]
**SYMMERS, ALEXANDER,** brewer in Dundee, 1748. [NAS.E326.1.50]
**SYMMERS, JOHN,** skipper in Dundee, 1748. [NAS.E326.1.50]
**TALBOT, JOHN,** weaver in Dundee, 1745. [JA]
**TAYLOR, ANDREW,** b.1752, maltman in Dundee, d. 1801, wife Elizabeth Boick. [HMI]
**TAYLOR, JAMES,** writer in Dundee, testament, 1731, CB.
**TEASDALE, JOHN,** Episcopal minister in Dundee, testament, 1785, CB. [NAS]
**THAIN, ANDREW,** brewer in Dundee, 1748. [NAS.E326.1.50]
**THAIN, JAMES,** in Dundee, testament, 1779, CB. [NAS]
**THAIN, PATRICK,** brewer in Dundee, 1748; testament, 1777, CB. [NAS.E326.1.50]
**THOM, DAVID,** merchant in Dundee, 1774. [NAS.CS16.1.157/403]
**THOM, JOHN,** merchant in Dundee, widow Margaret Nichol, children Margaret & John, 1707. [NAS.AC9.247]
**THOM. WILLIAM,** merchant in Dundee, testament, 1781, CB.

# THE PEOPLE OF DUNDEE, 1700-1799

**THOMAS, GEORGE,** manufacturer in Dundee, 1788. [NAS.SC20.36.15]

**THOMS, ALEXANDER,** of Rumgally, b.1730, merchant & provost of Dundee, d.1809, wife Grace Wise, b.1763, d.1847. [HMI]

**THOMS, JAMES,** shoemaker in Chapelshade, husb& of Margaret Cathro, b. 1725, d. 1788. [HMI]

**THOMSON, ANDREW,** merchant in Dundee, spouse Christian Baillie, b. 1679, d. 1746. [HMI]

**THOMSON, GILBERT,** in Dundee, 1748. [NAS.E326.1.50]

**THOMSON, HENRY,** merchant in Dundee, 1737, 1748. [NAS.AC9.1384; E326.1.50]

**THOMSON, JAMES,** of Eassie, merchant in Dundee, d. 1786, husband of Florinda Lawrie, b. 1738, d. 1772. [HMI]

**THOMSON, JOHN,** surgeon in Dundee, testament, 1747, CB.

**THOMSON, JOHN,** merchant in Dundee, 1748. [NAS.E326.1.50]

**THOMSON, JOHN,** baker in Dundee, 1799. [DCA.B19.3.27/159]

**THOMSON, JOHN,** b.1733, feuar in Lochee, d.1805. [HMI]

**THOMSON, PATRICK,** shoemaker in Dundee, 1745. [JA]

**THOMSON, WILLIAM,** carpenter in Dundee, 1740. [NAS.AC11.130]

**THORNTON, WILLIAM,** master of the Fame of Dundee, 1760s. [NAS.E504.11.6/7]

**TINDALL, JOHN,** writer in Dundee, testament, 1735, CB.

**TOD, ALEXANDER,** b.1710, vintner, d. 1762, wife Agnes Smith, b.1716, d.1779. [HMI]

**TOD, ANDREW,** merchant in Dundee, testament, 1733, CB.

**TOD, JOHN,** baker in Dundee, wife Elisabeth Mauer, b.1749, d.1798. [HMI]

**TOSHACH, ROBERT,** writer in Dundee, cashbook, 1752/1753. [NAS.CS96.1603]

**TRAILL, JOHN,** skipper in Dundee, 1748, testament, 1763, CB. [NAS.E326.1.50]

**TRAILL, THOMAS,** writer in Dundee, testament, 1752, 1756, CB. [NAS]

**URE, JOHN,** clerk to the Dundee Banking Company, 1783. [NRAS.124.4.2]

# THE PEOPLE OF DUNDEE, 1700-1799

**VALLANCE, ROBERT,** merchant in Dundee & Cupar, Fife, 1740s. [NRAS.NA#17321]

**WADDEL, JOHN,** maltman in Dundee, husband of Elisabeth Baxter, b. 1763, d. 1798. [HMI]

**WAGRIE, JOHN,** apprentice in Dundee, 1745. [JA]

**WAID, RICHARD,** b.1768 in Philadelphia, d.1787. [HMI]

**WALKER, ARCHIBALD,** Convenor in Dundee, 1748. [NAS.E326.1.50]

**WALKER, ARCHIBALD,** tanner in Dundee, testament, 1775, CB. [NAS]

**WALKER, DAVID,** merchant in Dundee, & co-owner of the Isobel & Betty of Dundee, 1745; testament, 1751, 1757, CB. [NAS.AC11.167]

**WALKER, DAVID,** weaver in Dundee, 1748. [NAS.E326.1.50]

**WALLACE, ROBERT,** skipper in North Ferry, testament, 1730, CB. [NAS]

**WANDLESS, ROBERT,** weaver in Dundee, testament, 1767, CB. [NAS]

**WARDEN, HUGH,** merchant trading between Dundee & Virginia, 1771. [NAS.E504.11.7]

**WARDROP, WILLIAM,** land-waiter in Dundee, testament, 1762, CB. [nas]

**WARDROPER, ANDREW,** seaman on the James of Dundee, 1716. [NAS.AC9.565]

**WARDROPER, ANDREW,** shoremaster of Dundee, 1725. [NAS.AC9.943]

**WARDROPER, ANDREW,** Provost of Dundee, 1748. [NAS.E326.1.50]

**WARDROPER, GEORGE,** master of the Betty of Dundee, 1725, testament, 1768, CB. [NAS.AC9.885]

**WARDROPER, GEORGE,** skipper in Dundee, father of Elizabeth, 1770. [NAS.CS16.1.141/190]

**WARDROPER, ROBERT,** merchant in Dundee, testament, 1714, CB. [NAS.AC9.503]

**WARDROPER, ROBERT,** shipmaster in Dundee & co-owner of the Newmarket Frigate, 1750; testament, 1768, CB. [NRAS.NA#10409]

**WARDROPER, THOMAS,** merchant & bailie of Dundee, part-owner of the James of Dundee, 1714/1716. [NAS.AC11.12; AC9.540/563]

# THE PEOPLE OF DUNDEE, 1700-1799

**WATSON, ALEXANDER,** b. 1737, mariner in Dundee, d. 1797, husband of Ann Adam, b. 1749, d. 1819. [HMI]
**WATSON, ALEXANDER,** in Dundee, 1748. [NAS.E326.1.50]
**WATSON, DAVID,** mason in Dundee, testament, 1723, CB; wife Mary Bruce, b.1650, d.1710. [HMI]
**WATSON, DAVID,** b.1715, wright in Hawkhill, d.1817, wife Isabella Lowrance, b.1755, d.1818. [HMI]
**WATSON, DAVID,** b. 1737, merchant in Murraygate, d. 1808. [HMI]
**WATSON, GEORGE,** merchant in Dundee, 1710. [NAS.AC9.359]
**WATSON, HENRY,** b.1708, smith in Dundee, 1748, d.1763. [NAS.E326.1.50][HMI]
**WATSON, JAMES,** baker in Wellgate, Dundee, 1796. [DCA.B19.3.26/1]
**WATSON, JOHN,** clerk to Thomas Davidson a writer in Dundee, 1788. [NRAS.124.4.2.56]
**WATSON, JOHN,** b. 1745, rector of Dundee Grammar School, d. 1809 in Glasgow, wife Elisabeth Campbell, b. 1745, d. 1797. [HMI]
**WATSON, ROBERT,** merchant in Dundee, 1706. [NAS.AC9.216]
**WATSON, ROBERT,** shoemaker in Dundee, testament, 1796, CB. [NAS]
**WATSON, THOMAS,** & Co., merchants in Dundee, 1731, 1739. [NAS.AC8.434; NRAS.150.3.20]
**WATSON, THOMAS,** messenger in Dundee, testament, 1778, CB. [NAS]
**WATSON, Captain WILLIAM,** in Dundee, 1748, testament, 1773, CB. [NAS.E326.1.50]
**WATT. ALEXANDER,** b.1706, maltman in Dundee, d. 1739, wife Ann Anderson, b. 1712, d.1764. [HMI]
**WATT, ALEXANDER,** merchant in Dundee, testament, 1784, CB. [NAS]
**WATT, JAMES,** weaver in Dundee, testament, 1733, CB. [NAS]
**WATT, JOHN,** barber in Dundee, testament, 1755, CB. [NAS]
**WATT, JOHN,** wright in Dundee, relict Catherine Turpie, testament, 1781, CB. [NAS]
**WAUGH, JAMES,** seaman on the James of Dundee, 1716. [NAS.AC9.565]

# THE PEOPLE OF DUNDEE, 1700-1799

**WEBSTER, DAVID,** master of the Speedwell of North Ferry of Dundee, 1716. [NAS.AC9.563]
**WEBSTER, DAVID,** carpenter in Dundee, testament, 1728, CB.
**WEBSTER, GEORGE,** in Dundee, 1748. [NAS.E326.1.50]
**WEBSTER, JAMES,** merchant from Dundee who settled in Jamaica by 1780. [DA.TC.CC15.91]
**WEBSTER, ROBERT,** skipper in North Ferry, testament, 1760, CB. [NAS]
**WEBSTER, THOMAS,** master of the Isobel of Dundee, 1741. [NAS.AC11.133]
**WEBSTER, THOMAS,** dyer in Dundee, 1748. [NAS.E326.1.50]
**WEBSTER, THOMAS,** late hospital master of Dundee, 1793. [DCA.B19.3.26/1]
**WEBSTER, WILLIAM,** slater in Dundee, 1798. [DCA.B19.3.27/2]
**WEDDERBURN, ALEXANDER,** town clerk of Dundee, 1715. [DCA.TC.CC.1/132]
**WEDDERBURN, ALEXANDER,** skipper in Dundee, testament, 1740, CB. [NAS]
**WEDDERBURN, Mrs GRIZEL,** in Dundee, 1748. [NAS.E326.1.50]
**WEDDERBURN, Dr JOHN,** in Dundee, 1748. [NAS.E326.1.50]
**WEDDERBURN, Mrs,** in Dundee, 1748. [NAS.E326.1.50]
**WEMYSS, JAMES,** skipper in Dundee, testament, 1750, CB.
**WEMYSS, JOHN,** merchant in Dundee, testament, 1800, CB.
**WEMYSS, JOHN,** weaver in Dundee, 1748. [NAS.E326.1.50]
**WEMYSS, THOMAS,** merchant in Dundee, 1797. [NAS.CS97.172.88]
**WEMYSS, WALTER,** merchant in Dundee, 1797. [NAS.CS97.172.88]
**WEST, HENRY,** waulker in Dundee, testament, 1747, CB.
**WHITE, EUPHAME,** relict of William Carmichael gardener in Dundee, testament, 1761, 1766, CB. [NAS]
**WHITE, MARGARET,** relict of Andrew Henderson chapman in Dundee, testament, 1718, CB. [NAS]
**WHITTET, ALISON,** relict of Patrick Williamson a skipper in Dundee, testament, 1751, 1757, CB. [NAS]
**WHITTIT, JOHN,** merchant in Dundee, testament, 1741, 1745, CB. [nas]
**WHYTE, ROBERT,** in Dundee, 1748. [NAS.E326.1.50]

# THE PEOPLE OF DUNDEE, 1700-1799

**WIGHTON, JAMES,** manufacturer in Dundee, testament, 1798, CB. [NAS]
**WILKIE, GEORGE,** merchant in Dundee, 1791, 1798. [DCA.B19.3.27/262][NAS.SC20.33.13]
**WILKIE, ROBERT,** b.1734, wright in Dundee, sasine, 1770, d.1827, wife (1) Elisabeth Fyfe, b.1739, d.1787, (2) Elisabeth Herald, b.1767, d.1826. [NAS.RS35. 67][HMI]
**WILKIE, THOMAS,** surgeon apothecary in Dundee, 1715. [NAS.E650.53]
**WILKIE, WILLIAM,** in Hilltown, sasine, 1704. [NAS.RS35.10.624]
**WILL, ANDREW,** clerk to the Town Clerk of Dundee, 1798.. [DCA.B19.3.27/6]
**WILL, JAMES,** b.1684, merchant tailor in Dundee, d.1754. [HMI]
**WILLIAMSON, DAVID,** merchant in Dundee, 1745. [JA]
**WILLIAMSON, JOHN,** cooper in Dundee, 1745. [JA]
**WILLIAMSON, PATRICK,** merchant in Dundee, 1748, testament, 1752, CB. [NAS.E326.1.50]
**WILLIAMSON, PETER,** b. 1741, d. 1810. [HMI]
**WILLISON, Dr ANDREW,** in Dundee, 1748, testament, 1768, CB. [NAS.E326.1.50]
**WILLISON, DAVID,** merchant in Dundee, 1748. [NAS.E326.1.50]
**WILLISON, Reverend JOHN,** in Dundee, 1748. [NAS.E326.1.50]
**WILSON, ALEXANDER,** maltman in Dundee, testament, 1719, CB. [NAS]
**WINTER, WILLIAM,** b. 1706, vintner in Dundee, d. 1756, husband of Isobel Key. [HMI]
**WINTER, WILLIAM,** horse hirer in Dundee, sasine, 1741. [NAS.RS35.16.39]
**WISHART, JEAN,** in Dundee, testament, 1798, CB. [NAS]
**WISHART, JOHN,** merchant in Dundee, 1745. [JA]
**WOOD, JAMES,** skipper in Dundee, testament, 1773, CB.
**WOOD, WILLIAM,** mason in Dundee, 1745. [JA]
**WRIGHT, ALEXANDER,** merchant in Dundee, 1748; testament, 1771, 1779, CB. [NAS.E326.1.50]
**WRIGHT, GEORGE,** merchant in Dundee, testament, 1774, CB.

# THE PEOPLE OF DUNDEE, 1700-1799

**WRIGHT, JAMES,** jr., merchant in Dundee, 1791.
[DCA.B19.3.27/262]
**YEAMAN, ELIZABETH,** relict in Dundee, testament, 1711, CB.
**YEAMAN, Captain GEORGE,** merchant in Dundee, 1714.
[NAS.RD4.89.416]
**YEAMAN, GEORGE,** bailie in Dundee, 1748. [NAS.E326.1.50]
**YEAMAN, ISABEL,** relict of George Proffit a merchant in Dundee, testament, 1778, CB.
**YEAMAN, JAMES,** merchant in Dundee, 1714, bailie in 1718; testament, 1752, CB. [NAS.AC11.12; B59.30.46]
**YEAMAN, JEAN,** spouse of Rev, Robert Smith in Dundee, testament, 1776, CB.
**YEAMAN, KATHERINE,** daughter of James Yeaman a merchant in Dundee, testament, 1783, CB. [nas]
**YEAMAN, PATRICK,** b.1697, provost of Dundee, 1748, d.1767; testament, 1770, 1773, CB. [NAS.E326.1.50][HMI]
**YEAMAN, PATRICK,** in Dundee, testament, 1781, CB. [NAS]
**YEAMAN, WILLIAM,** of Balbeuchly, merchant in Dundee, son of the late George Yeaman a merchant & Provost of Dundee, 1790; 1799.
[NAS.SC20.36.15][DCA.B19.3.27/253]
**YEAMAN, Madam,** in Dundee, 1748. [NAS.E326.1.50]
**YEAMAN, Miss,** in Dundee, 1748. [NAS.E326.1.50]
**YOUNG, ARCHIBALD,** in Dundee, 1748; testament, 1762, CB.
[NAS.E326.1.50]
**YOUNG, JAMES,** servant in Dundee, 1745. [JA]
**YOUNG, JAMES,** b. 1695, merchant in Dundee, d. 1755, wife Margaret Thomson, b. 1701, d. 1755. [HMI]
**YOUNG, JAMES,** surgeon in Dundee, testament, 1778, CB.
**YOUNG, JAMES,** skipper in Dundee, testament, 1798, CB.
**YOUNG, JOHN,** skipper in Dundee, 1704. [NAS.AC9.51]
**YOUNG, JOHN,** mariner in North Ferry, testament, 1738, CB.
**YOUNG, WILLIAM,** merchant in Dundee, 1738.
[NAS.AC10.255]
**YOUNGER, JAMES,** merchant in Dundee, 1711.
[NAS.AC9.406]

www.ingramcontent.com/pod-product-compliance
Lightning Source LLC
Chambersburg PA
CBHW072200160426
43197CB00012B/2467